THE
COMPOUND
EFFECT

MULTIPLYING YOUR SUCCESS. ONE SIMPLE STEP AT A TIME.

This book is being given to

_____

because I care about you and your greater success,

_____

Also by Darren Hardy

*Design Your Best Year Ever: A Proven Formula
for Achieving BIG GOALS*

*Living Your Best Year Ever: A Proven System
for Achieving BIG GOALS*

Praise for *The Compound Effect*

"This powerful, practical book, based on years of proven and profitable experience, shows you how to leverage your special talents to maximize the opportunities surrounding you. The Compound Effect is a treasure chest of ideas for achieving greater success than you ever thought possible!"

—Brian Tracy, speaker and author of *The Way to Wealth*

"A brilliant formula for living an extraordinary life. Read it, and most important, take action upon it!"

—Jack Canfield, co-author of *The Success Principles: How to Get from Where You Are to Where You Want to Be*

"Darren Hardy has written a new bible for the self-improvement space. If you are looking for the real deal—a real program, with real tools that can change your life and make your dreams a reality—The Compound Effect is it! I plan to use this book to go back and look at what I need to again work on in my own life! Buy ten copies, one for yourself and nine more for those you love, and pass them out now—those who get it will thank you!

—David Bach, founder of FinishRich.com and author of eight *New York Times* best-sellers, including *The Automatic Millionaire*

"This book will enable you to climb the ladder of success two steps at a time. Buy it, read it, and bank it."

—Jeffrey Gitomer, author of *The Sales Bible* and *The Little Red Book of Selling*

"Darren Hardy is in a unique position to aggregate the brainpower of the most successful people in the world and boil it down to what really matters. Simple, direct, and to the point—these are the principles that have guided my life and every top business leader I know. This book will show you the way to your own greater success, happiness, and fulfillment."

—Donny Deutsch, television host and chairman of Deutsch, Inc.

"The Compound Effect *is a brilliant formula for achieving the life of your dreams. Step by step, let it be your guide. Read and study it, but most important, put it into action!*"

—Chris Widener, speaker and author of *The Art of Influence: Persuading Others Begins with You* and *The Twelve Pillars*

"Darren Hardy proves with The Compound Effect *that common sense— when applied—yields amazingly uncommon results. Follow these simple steps and become who you were meant to be!*"

—Denis Waitley, speaker and author of *The Psychology of Winning*

"The Compound Effect *will help you beat the competition, rise above your challenges, and create the life you deserve!*"

—T. Harv Eker, author of the No. 1 *New York Times* best-seller *Secrets of the Millionaire Mind*

"Einstein said, 'Compounding is the eighth wonder of the world.' To compound your successes, read, apprehend, comprehend, and fully use my friend Darren Hardy's brilliance to realize all your dreams, hopes, and desires."

—Mark Victor Hansen, co-creator of the No. 1 *New York Times* best-selling series *Chicken Soup for the Soul* and co-author of *The One Minute Millionaire*

"People who talk about 'success' but don't find ways to translate it into their personal lives—into their relationships and their marriages and their families— do not win my respect or my admiration. In fact, their words ring hollow. As long as we have known Darren Hardy, we have never had a conversation where we have not talked about our kids, about our wives, and about how our families are doing. We think Darren knows a lot about achieving success, and even more important, he wants people to achieve it for the right reasons!"

—Richard and Linda Eyre, authors of the *New York Times* No. 1 best-selling *Teaching Your Children Values*

"Daren Hardy's The Compound Effect *is a culmination of success principles that is relevant to anyone who needs it! As a thought leader, he is making a significant contribution to our industry. A wonderful book!*"

—Stedman Graham, author, speaker, entrepreneur

"From time to time, you get the opportunity to make the leap from where you now are to where you've always wanted to be. This book is that opportunity. And now is your time. A superb work from a leading light."

—Robin Sharma, author of the No. 1 best-sellers *The Monk Who Sold His Ferrari* and *The Leader Who Had No Title*

"I have spent a lifetime helping people get to the bottom line so that they can be successful and achieve instant results, which is why I absolutely love this book and recommend it to all of my clients. Darren has an amazing gift for sharing powerful techniques and telling it like it is so that you can save valuable time and get right to work putting his formula for success into action immediately."

—Connie Podesta, keynote speaker, author and executive coach

"If anyone knows the fundamentals of success, it's Darren Hardy, publisher and editorial director of SUCCESS magazine! This book is about a return and focus on the basics, what it really takes to earn success. Make The Compound Effect *your operations manual for life—one simple step at a time!"*

—Dr. Tony Alessandra, author of *The Platinum Rule* and *Charisma*

"With The Compound Effect, *Darren Hardy has joined the ranks of the great self-improvement authors! If you are serious about success and living your true potential, reading this book is a must. It will serve as your operations manual for success."*

—Vic Conant, chairman of Nightingale-Conant

"Life is fast with lots of distractions. If you want to advance effectively, don't just read this book—study it with a highlighter."

—Tony Jeary, coach to the world's top CEOs and high-achievers

"SUCCESS magazine has been a fountain of powerful ideas since the day it was launched over a century ago. Now, Darren Hardy, the journal's 21st-century steward, has distilled the essential fundamentals you'll need to create the life you've always imagined. You shouldn't read this book—you should devour it from cover to cover."

—Steve Farber, author of the best-sellers *The Radical Leap* and *Greater Than Yourself*

"This is a must-read book for success seekers. You want to know what it takes? You want to know what to do? It's all here. This is your operation manual for success.
—Keith Ferrazzi, No. 1 *New York Times* best-selling author of *Who's Got Your Back* and *Never Eat Alone*

"The Compound Effect *is a powerful, comprehensive guide to success. It gives a complete strategy to get you from where you are to where you want to be. The name Darren Hardy means success! My advice is read the book, do the work, and achieve success."*
—Jeffrey Hayzlett, author of *The Mirror Test* and CMO of Kodak

"You can take the rest of your life and try to figure out how to achieve success, or you can follow the proven and tested principals and methods found in this book. It's your choice, do it the hard way... or do it the smart way!"
—John Assaraf, author of *The Answer* and *Having It All*

"Finally! Darren Hardy has done it with this book. It's a terrific distillation of the essential fundamentals needed to achieve the life you've always imagined. Master these basics, and you will be the master of your future!"
—Don Hutson, speaker, co-author of the No. 1 *New York Times* best-selling *The One Minute Entrepreneur*, and CEO of U.S. Learning

"Your life will be the net result of each step you take. Let this powerful guide show you how to make better choices, develop better habits, and think better thoughts. Your success is truly in your hands... in this book."
—Jim Cathcart, speaker and author of *The Acorn Principle*

"At Zappos, one of our core values is to Pursue Growth and Learning. In the lobby of our headquarters, we have a giving library where we give away books to employees and visitors that we think will help with their growth, both personally and professionally. I can't wait to add The Compound Effect *to our library."*
—Tony Hsieh, author of *Delivering Happiness* and CEO of Zappos

"If there were ever a person who has his finger on the pulse of success, it's Darren Hardy, publisher and editorial director of SUCCESS *magazine. I always look forward to reading what he has to say. He is a great synthesizer of great ideas."*
—Larry Benet, chairman of the Speakers and Authors Networking Group

THE
COMPOUND
EFFECT

MULTIPLYING YOUR SUCCESS. ONE SIMPLE STEP AT A TIME.

DARREN HARDY
— Publisher *SUCCESS* magazine

Vanguard Press
A Member of the Perseus Books Group

Published by Vanguard Press
A Member of the Perseus Books Group

Reprinted by arrangement with SUCCESS Books™, an imprint of SUCCESS Media.

Cataloging-in-Publication data for this book is available from the Library of Congress.

ISBN 978-1-59315-713-5 (hardcover)
ISBN 978-1-59315-724-1 (paperback)
ISBN 978-1-59315-714-2 (e-book)

Vanguard Press books are available at special discounts for bulk purchases in the U.S. by corporations, institutions, and other organizations. For more information, please contact the Special Markets Department at the Perseus Books Group, 2300 Chestnut Street, Suite 200, Philadelphia, PA 19103, or call (800) 810-4145, ext. 5000, or e-mail special.markets@perseusbooks.com.

20 19 18 17 16 15 14 13 12 11

This book is dedicated to:

Jerry Hardy, my best man, my dad: the man who taught me the principles of the Compound Effect through his example.

And, to Jim Rohn, my mentor: the man who taught me, amongst many things, to talk about things that matter to people who care.

WARNING! These chapter headings look simple. Success strategies are no longer a secret, but most people ignore them. You think you already know the secret to success? So does everyone else. But the six strategies within this book, when applied in sequence, will launch your income, your life — your success — like nothing before.

As the publisher of *SUCCESS* magazine, I've seen it all. Nothing works like the power of the **Compound Effect** of simple actions done right over time.

This is it, the real deal on what it takes to achieve massive success in your life. Whatever your dream, desire, or goal in life, the plan to achieve it all is found in the book you're holding. Read on, and let it rock your world.

CONTENTS

ACKNOWLEDGMENTS

I extend my appreciation and thanks to my team at SUCCESS Media and *SUCCESS* magazine, who have supported me through this labor of blood, sweat, and almost tears, particularly my good friends and colleagues Reed Bilbray and Stuart Johnson...

To my writing muse and collaborator, Linda Sivertsen, who helped pull out the stories and references from my past and give my process order and coherence...

To the editing wizardry of Erin Casey, the always-genius touch of our *SUCCESS* magazine editor Lisa Ocker, and to our editor in chief, Deborah Heisz...

To the many brilliant personal-development experts I have worked with and learned from over the past two decades—all the CEOs, revolutionary entrepreneurs, and extraordinary achievers I have had the chance to interview and glean new insights, ideas, and wisdom from...

To all the readers of *SUCCESS* magazine, my blog, and my other works, and whose enthusiastic and appreciative feedback inspires me to want to continue to pursue the zenith of my potential, so I can better assist others to find theirs...

And finally, and most important, to my beautiful and wonderful wife, Georgia, who sacrificed many late nights and weekends without me while I worked to complete this manuscript.

No matter what you learn,
what strategy or tactic you employ,
success comes as the result of
the Compound Effect.

SPECIAL MESSAGE FROM ANTHONY ROBBINS

During the past three decades, I've had the privilege of helping more than 4 million people create breakthroughs in their lives. I've worked with an immensely diverse group of people—from presidents of countries to prisoners, Olympic athletes, and Oscar-winning entertainers, from billionaire entrepreneurs to those just struggling to start their own business. Whether working with a couple fighting to keep their family together or a person in prison searching for a way to change their life from the inside out, my focus has always been on helping people achieve real and *sustainable* results. You can't do that through a magic pill or secret formula, but *only* through understanding the real tools, strategies, and science behind what it takes to break through the patterns that defeat so many and achieve a meaningful life.

Darren and I both made the decision to take control of our lives at an early age. We searched for answers by seeking out people who were living the kind of life we wanted to live. Then we applied what we learned. It's not really all that surprising that we both cite Jim Rohn as a mentor. Jim was a master at helping people understand the truths, the laws, and the practices that lead to real, lasting success. Jim taught us that achievement is not about luck; it's really a science. Sure, everyone is different, but the same laws of success always apply. You reap what you sow; you can't get out of life what you're not willing to put into it. If you want more love, give more love. If you want greater success, help others achieve more. And when you study and master the science of achievement, you will find the success you desire.

Darren Hardy is living proof of this philosophy. He walks the talk. What he shares in his book is based on what has worked in his life—and mine as well.

This is a guy who has taken simple but profound fundamentals of what it takes to be successful and used them to earn more than a million dollars a year by age twenty-four, and build a company to more than $50 million by age twenty-seven. For the past twenty years, his life has been a personal laboratory of study and research on the topic of success. He's used himself as a guinea pig, testing thousands of different ideas, resources, and tools, and through his failings and his triumphs, he's figured out which ideas and strategies have merit, and which ones are just plain BS.

For sixteen years, I have crossed paths with Darren, who as a leader in the personal-development industry, has worked closely with hundreds of top writers, speakers, and thought leaders. He has trained tens of thousands of entrepreneurs, advised many large companies, and personally mentored dozens of top CEOs and high-performance achievers, extracting from them what really matters and really works, and what doesn't. In his role as publisher of *SUCCESS* magazine, Darren sits at the center of the personal development industry. He's interviewed top leaders, from Richard Branson to General Colin Powell to Lance Armstrong, on a multitude of success topics, and drilled down to their best ideas, compiling them all—even a few of mine. He is an all-consuming, sorting, filtering, digesting, analyzing, summarizing, categorizing, itemizing, personal-achievement encyclopedia of information. He has culled the clutter, and focused on the core fundamentals that matter—fundamentals that you can immediately implement in *your* life to produce measurable and sustainable results.

The Compound Effect is the operator's manual that teaches you how to own the system, how to control it, master it, and shape it to your needs and desires. Once you do, there is nothing you can't obtain or achieve.

The Compound Effect is based on a principle I've used in my own life and training; that is, your decisions shape your destiny. The future is what you make of it. Little, everyday decisions will either take you to the life you desire or to disaster by default. In fact, it's the littlest decisions that shape our lives. Stray off course by just two millimeters, and your trajectory changes; what seemed like a tiny, inconsequential decision then can become a mammoth miscalculation now. From what to eat and where to work, to the people you spend your time with, to how you spend your afternoon, every choice shapes how you live today, but more important, how you live the rest of your life. But the good news is, change is within you. In the same way a two-millimeter miscalculation can send you veering wildly off your life's course, a mere two-millimeter readjustment can also bring you right back home. The trick is finding the plan, the guide, the map that shows you where that home is. How you get there. How you stay on the path.

This book *is* that detailed, tangible plan of action. Let it shake up your expectations, eliminate your assumptions, ignite your curiosity, and bring value to your life—starting right *now*. Take advantage of this tool. Use it as a guide to create the life and the success you want. If you do this, and if you do all the other right things—and keep doing them day in and day out—I know you will experience the best life has to offer.

Live with passion!

Anthony Robbins
Entrepreneur, author and peak-performance strategist

INTRODUCTION

This book is about success and what it really takes to earn it. It's time someone told it to you straight. You've been bamboozled for too long. There is no magic bullet, secret formula, or quick fix. You don't make $200,000 a year spending two hours a day on the Internet, lose 30 pounds in a week, rub 20 years off your face with a cream, fix your love life with a pill, or find lasting success with any other scheme that is too good to be true. It would be great if you could buy your success, fame, self-esteem, good relationships, and health and well-being in a nicely clam-shelled package at the local Walmart. But, that's not how it works.

We are constantly bombarded with increasingly sensational claims to get rich, get fit, get younger, get sexier… all overnight with little effort for only three easy payments of $39.95. These repetitive marketing messages have distorted our sense of what it really takes to succeed. We've lost sight of the simple but profound fundamentals of what it takes to be successful.

I'm tired of it. I won't sit back and watch these reckless messages derail people any longer. I wrote this book to take you back to basics. I'm going to help you clear the clutter and bring focus to the core fundamentals that matter. You can immediately implement in *your* life the exercises and time-tested success principles this book contains to produce measurable and sustainable results. I'm going to teach you to harness the power of the Compound Effect, the operating system that has been running your life, for better or worse. Use this system to your advantage and you truly can revolutionize your life. You have heard you can achieve anything you set your mind to, right? Well, only if you know how. *The Compound Effect* is the operator's manual that teaches you how to master the system. When you do, there is nothing you can't obtain or achieve.

How do I know that the Compound Effect is the only process you need for ultimate success? Firstly, I have applied these principles to my own life. Now I hate it when authors beat their chests about their fame and fortune, but it's important you know I speak from personal experience—I'm offering you living proof, not regurgitated theory. As Anthony Robbins mentioned, I've enjoyed significant success in my business endeavors because I've made it a point to live by the principles you'll read in this book. For the past twenty years I've been intensely studying success and human achievement. I have spent hundreds of thousands of dollars testing thousands of different ideas, resources, and philosophies. My personal experience has proven that, no matter what you learn or what strategy or tactic you employ, success comes as the result of the operating system of the Compound Effect.

Secondly, for the past sixteen years I have been a leader in the personal-development industry. I've worked with respected thought leaders, speakers and authors. As a speaker and consultant, I've trained tens of thousands of entrepreneurs. I've mentored business leaders, corporate executives and countless high-achievers. From thousands of case studies I have extracted what works—and what doesn't.

Thirdly, as publisher of *SUCCESS* magazine, I sift through thousands of article submissions and books, help choose the experts we feature in the magazine, and review all of their material. Each month I interview a half-dozen top experts on a multitude of success topics and drill down to their best ideas. All day, every day, I read and filter through an ocean of personal-achievement information.

Here's my point. When you have such an exhaustive view of this industry, and wisdom gained through studying the teachings and best practices of some the world's most successful people, an amazing clarity emerges—the underlying fundamental truths become crystal clear. Having seen it, read it, and heard most all of it, I can no longer be fooled by the latest gambit or self-proclaimed prophet with the newest "scientific breakthrough." Nobody can sell me on gimmicks. I have too many reference points. I've gone down too many roads and learned the truth the hard way. As my mentor, the great business philosopher Jim Rohn, said, "There are no new fundamentals. Truth is not new; it's old. You've got to be a little suspicious of the guy who says, 'Come over here, I want to show you my manufactured antiques!' No, you can't manufacture antiques."

What this book is about, with all the unnecessary noise, fat, and fluff removed, is what really matters. What really works? What half-dozen basics, when focused on and mastered, constitute the operating system that can take you to any goal you desire and help you live the life you were meant to live? This book contains those half-dozen fundamentals; they comprise the operating system called *the Compound Effect*.

Before we dig in, I have one warning: Earning success is hard. The process is laborious, tedious, sometimes even boring. Becoming wealthy, influential, and world-class in your field is slow and arduous. Don't get me wrong; you'll see results in your life from following these steps almost immediately. But if you have an aversion to work, discipline, and commitment, you're welcome to turn the TV back on and put your hope in the next infomercial—the one touting promises of overnight success, if you have access to a major credit card.

Here's the bottom line: You already know all that you need to succeed. You don't need to learn anything more. If all we needed was more information, everyone with an Internet connection would live in a mansion, have abs of steel, and be blissfully happy. New or more information is *not* what you need—a new plan of *action* is. It's time to create new behaviors and habits that are oriented away from sabotage and toward success. It's that simple.

Throughout the book I mention resources I've made available at TheCompoundEffect.com. Please, go there! Use them! This book and the tools I've provided to support you offer the best of everything I've heard, seen, studied, and tried. It's the best of what we bring you every month in *SUCCESS* magazine, all in one life-changing little book. And it *is* simple!

Let's get started!

CHAPTER 1

THE COMPOUND EFFECT IN ACTION

You know that expression, "Slow and steady wins the race"? Ever heard the story of the tortoise and the hare? Ladies and gentlemen, I'm the tortoise. Give me enough time, and I will beat virtually anybody, anytime, in any competition. Why? Not because I'm the best or the smartest or the fastest. I'll win because of the positive habits I've developed, and because of the consistency I use in applying those habits. I'm the world's biggest believer in consistency. I'm living proof that it's the ultimate key to success, yet it's one of the biggest pitfalls for people struggling to achieve. Most people don't know how to sustain it. I do. I have my father to thank for that. In essence, he was my first coach for igniting the power of the Compound Effect.

My parents divorced when I was eighteen months old, and my dad raised me as a single father. He wasn't exactly the soft, nurturing type. He was a former university football coach, and he hard-wired me for achievement.

Thanks to Dad, wake-up calls were at six o'clock every morning. Not by a loving tap on the shoulder or even the sound of a radio alarm. No, I was awakened each morning by the repetitious pile-driving sound of iron pounding on the concrete floor of our garage, situated next to my bedroom. It was like waking up twelve feet from a construction zone. He'd painted a huge "No pain, no gain" sign on the wall of the garage, which he stared at while he did countless old-school strongman dead lifts, power cleans, lunges, and squats. Rain, sleet, or shine, Dad was out there in his shorts and tattered sweatshirt. He never missed a day. You could set your watch by his routine.

I had more chores than a housekeeper and gardener put together. Upon returning from school, there was always a list of instructions to greet me: pull weeds, rake leaves, sweep the garage, dust, vacuum, do the dishes—you name it. And getting behind in school wasn't tolerated. That's just the way it was.

Dad was the original "no excuses" guy. We weren't ever allowed to stay home from school sick, unless we were actually puking, bleeding, or "showing bone." The term "showing bone" came from his coaching days; his players knew they weren't allowed to come out of the game unless they were seriously injured. One time his quarterback asked to be pulled out of the game. Dad said, "Not unless you're showing bone." The quarterback pulled back his shoulder pads, and sure enough, his collarbone was showing. Only then was he allowed to come off the field.

One of Dad's core philosophies was, "It doesn't matter

how smart you are or aren't, you need to make up in hard work what you lack in experience, skill, intelligence, or innate ability. If your competitor is smarter, more talented, or experienced, you just need to work three or four times as hard. You can still beat them!" No matter what the challenge, he taught me to make up in hard work for wherever I might be disadvantaged. Miss free throws at the game? Do one thousand free throws every day for a month. Not good at dribbling with your left hand? Tie your right hand behind your back and dribble three hours a day. Behind in your math? Hunker down, hire a tutor, and work like hell all summer until you get it. No excuses. If you aren't good at something, work harder, work smarter. He walked his talk, too. Dad went from being a football coach to a top salesperson. From there he became the boss, and ultimately, went on to own his own company.

But I wasn't given loads of instruction. From the beginning, Dad let us figure it out. He was all about taking personal responsibility. He didn't hammer on us every night about homework; we just had to show up with the results. And, when you did, you were celebrated. If we got good grades, Dad took us to Prings, an ice cream parlor where you could get these king banana splits—six scoops of ice cream and all the fixings! Many times my siblings didn't fare as well in school, so they didn't get to go. Getting to go was a big deal, so you worked your butt off to win the trip.

Dad's discipline served as an example for me. Dad was my idol, and I wanted him to be proud of me. I also lived in fear of disappointing him. One of his philosophies is, "Be the guy who says 'no.' It's no great achievement to go along with the crowd. Be the unusual guy, the extraordinary guy." That's why I never did drugs—he never harped on me about it, but I didn't want to be that guy who just went along because everyone else was doing it. And I didn't want to let Dad down.

Thanks to Dad, by age 12, I'd mastered a schedule worthy of the most efficient CEO. Sometimes I griped and moaned (I was a kid!), but even then I secretly liked knowing that I had an edge over my classmates. Dad gave me a serious head start on the discipline and mentality it takes to be dedicated and responsible, to achieve whatever I set out to achieve. (It's no accident that the tagline of *SUCCESS* magazine is "What *Achievers* Read.")

Today, Dad and I joke about what an addictive overachiever he trained me to be. At eighteen, I was making a six-figure income in my own business. By age twenty, I owned my own home in an upscale neighborhood. By age twenty-four, my income grew to more than $1 million a year, and by age twenty-seven, I was officially a self-made millionaire with a business that brought in more than $50 million in revenue. That just about brings us to the present day, because I'm not yet forty, but I have enough money and assets to last my family the rest of my life.

"There are lots of ways to screw up a kid," Dad says. "At least my way was a pretty good one! You seemed to have done pretty well."

So, while I admit that I've had to *practice* sitting on my hands and being present in the moment, or chilling out peacefully in a beach chair from time to time (without taking a pile of business books or self-improvement CDs with me), I'm grateful for the success skills I learned from my dad, and my other mentors along the way.

The Compound Effect reveals the "secret" behind my success. I'm a true believer in the Compound Effect because Dad made sure that I lived it, each and every day, until I couldn't live any other way if I tried.

But if you're like most people, you're not a true believer. There are lots of perfectly understandable reasons why. You haven't had the same coaching and example showing you what to do. You haven't experienced the payoff of the Compound Effect. As a society, we have been deceived. We've been hypnotized by commercial marketing, which convinces you of problems you don't have and sells you on the idea of insta-fixes to "cure" them. We've been socialized to believe in the fairy-tale endings found in movies and novels. We've lost sight of the good, old-fashioned value of hard and consistent work.

Let's examine these hurdles one by one.

You Haven't Experienced the Payoff of the Compound Effect

The Compound Effect is the principle of reaping huge rewards from a series of small, smart choices. What's most interesting about this process to me is that, even though the results are massive, the steps, in the moment, don't *feel* significant. Whether you're using this strategy for improving your health, relationships, finances, or anything else for that matter, the changes are so subtle, they're almost imperceptible. These small changes offer little or no immediate result, no big win, no obvious I-told-you-so payoff. So why bother?

Most people get tripped up by the simplicity of the Compound Effect. For instance, they quit after the eighth day of running because they're still overweight. Or, they stop practicing the piano after six months because they haven't mastered anything other than "Chopsticks." Or, they stop making contributions to their IRA after a few years because they could use the cash—and it doesn't seem to be adding up to much anyway.

What they don't realize is that these small, seemingly insignificant steps completed consistently over time will create a radical difference. Let me give you a few detailed examples.

Small, Smart Choices + Consistency + Time = RADICAL DIFFERENCE

The Magic Penny

If you were given a choice between taking $3 million in cash this very instant and a single penny that doubles in value every day for 31 days, which would you choose? If you've heard this before, you know the penny gambit is the choice you should make—you know it's the course that will lead to greater wealth. Yet why is it so hard to believe choosing the penny will result in more money in the end? *Because it takes so much longer to see the payoff.* Let's take a closer look.

Let's say you take the cold, hard cash and your friend goes the penny route. On Day Five, your friend has sixteen cents. You, however, have $3 million. On Day Ten, it's $5.12 versus your big bucks. How do you think your friend is feeling about her decision? You're spending your millions, enjoying the heck out of it, and loving your choice.

After 20 full days, with only 11 days left, Penny Lane has only $5,243. How is she feeling about herself at this point? For all her sacrifice and positive behavior, she has barely more than $5,000. You, however, have $3 million. Then the invisible magic of the Compound Effect starts to become visible. The same small mathematical growth improvement each day makes the compounded penny worth $10,737,418.24 on Day Thirty-one, more than three times your $3 million.

In this example we see why consistency over time is so important. On Day Twenty-nine, you've got your $3 million; Penny Lane has around $2.7 million. It isn't until Day Thirty of this 31-day race that she pulls ahead, with $5.3 million. And it isn't until the *very last day* of this monthlong ultramarathon that your friend blows you out of the water; she ends up with $10,737,418.24 to your $3 million.

Very few things are as impressive as the "magic" of compounding pennies. Amazingly, this "force" is equally powerful in every area of your life.

Here's another example...

Three Friends

Let's take three buddies who all grew up together. They live in the same neighborhood, with very similar sensibilities. Each makes around $50,000 a year. They're all married and have average health and body weight, plus a little bit of that dreaded "marriage flab."

Friend number one, let's call him Larry, plods along doing as he's always done. He's happy, or so he thinks, but complains occasionally that nothing ever changes.

Friend number two, Scott, starts making some small, seemingly inconsequential, positive changes. He begins reading 10 pages of a good book per day and listening to

30 minutes of something instructional or inspirational on his commute to work. Scott wants to see changes in his life, but doesn't want to make a fuss over it. He recently read an interview with Dr. Mehmet Oz in *SUCCESS* magazine and chose one idea from the article to implement in his life: He's going to cut 125 calories from his diet every day. No big deal. We're talking maybe a cup of cereal less, trading that can of soda for a bottle of seltzer, switching from mayo to mustard on his sandwich. Doable. He's also started walking a couple thousand extra steps per day (less than a mile). No grand acts of bravery or effort. Stuff anyone could do. But Scott is determined to stick with these choices, knowing that even though they're simple, he could also easily be tempted to abandon them.

Friend number three, Brad, makes a few poor choices. He recently bought a new big-screen TV so he can watch more of his favorite programs. He's been trying out the recipes he's seen on the Food Channel—the cheesy casseroles and desserts are his favorites. Oh, and he installed a bar in his family room and added one alcoholic drink per week to his diet. Nothing crazy; Brad just wants to have a little more fun.

At the end of five months, no perceivable differences exist among Larry, Scott, or Brad. Scott continues to read a little bit every night and listen to audios during his commute; Brad is "enjoying" life and doing less. Larry keeps doing as he always has. Even though each man has his own pattern of behavior, five months isn't long enough to see any real decline or improvement in their situations. In fact, if you charted the three men's weights, you'd see a rounding error of zero. They'd look exactly equal.

At the end of ten months, we still can't see noticeable changes in any of their lives. It's not until we get to the end of the eighteenth month that the slightest differences are measurable in these three friends' appearances.

But at about month twenty-five, we start seeing really measurable, visible differences. At month twenty-seven, we see an expansive difference. And, by month thirty-one, the change is startling. Brad is now fat while Scott is trim. By simply cutting 125 calories a day, in thirty-one months, Scott has lost thirty-three pounds!

---

31 months = 940 days

940 days x 125 calories/day = 117,500 calories

117,500 calories divided by 3500 calories per pound = 33.5 pounds!

Brad ate only 125 more calories more a day in that same time frame, and gained 33.5 pounds. Now he weighs 67 pounds more than Scott! But the differences are more significant than weight. Scott's invested almost one thousand hours reading good books and listening to self-improvement audios; by putting his newly gained knowledge into practice, he's earned a promotion and a raise. Best of all, his marriage is thriving. Brad? He's unhappy at work, and his marriage is on the rocks. And Larry? Larry is pretty much exactly where he was two and half years ago, except now he's a little more bitter about it.

The phenomenal power of the Compound Effect is that simple. The difference between people who employ the Compound Effect for their benefit compared to their peers who allow the same effect to work against them is almost inconceivable. It looks miraculous! Like magic or quantum leaps. After thirty-one months (or thirty-one years), the person who uses the positive nature of the Compound Effect appears to be an "overnight success." In reality, his or her profound success was the result of small, smart choices, completed consistently over time.

The Ripple Effect

The results in the above example seem dramatic, I know. But it goes even deeper than that. The reality is that even one small change can have a significant impact that causes an unexpected and unintended ripple effect. Let's put one of Brad's bad habits under the microscope—eating rich food more frequently—to better understand how the Compound Effect can also work in a negative way and can create a ripple effect that impacts your entire life.

Brad makes some muffins from a recipe he learned from the Food Channel. He's proud and his family loves it, and it seems to add value all around. He starts making them (and other sweets) frequently. He loves his own cooking and eats more than his share—but not so much that anyone notices. However, the extra food makes Brad sluggish at night. He wakes up a little groggy, which makes him cranky. The crankiness and sleep-deprivation begin to impact his work performance. He's less productive, and as a result, gets discouraging feedback from his boss. By the end of the day, he feel dissatisfied with his job and his energy level is way down. The commute home seems longer and more stressful than ever. All of this makes him reach for more comfort food—stress has a way of doing that.

The overall lack of energy makes Brad less likely to

take walks with his wife, like he used to. He just doesn't feel like it. She misses their time together and takes his withdrawal personally. With fewer shared activities with his wife and an absence of fresh air and exercise, Brad's not getting the endorphin release that had helped make him feel upbeat and enthusiastic. Because he's not as happy, he starts finding fault with himself and others, and stops complimenting his wife. As his own body starts to feel flabby, he feels less self-confident, less attractive and becomes less romantic.

Brad doesn't realize how his lack of energy and affection toward his wife affects her. He just knows that he feels funky. He starts losing himself in late-night TV because it's easy and distracting. Feeling his distance, Brad's wife starts to complain, then becomes needy. When that doesn't work, she emotionally withdraws to protect herself. She's lonely. She pours her energy into her work and spends more time with her girlfriends to fulfill her need for companionship. Men start flirting with her, which makes her feel desirable again. She would never cheat on Brad, but he has a feeling something's wrong. Instead of seeing that *his* poor choices and behaviors are at the root of their problems, he finds fault with his wife.

Believing that the *other* person is wrong rather than looking inside and doing the work necessary to clean up your mess is basic Psychology 101 stuff. In Brad's case, he doesn't know to look inside—they don't offer self-improvement or relationship advice on *Top Chef* or his favorite crime shows. However, the thought may have occurred to him that, if he had read the personal-development books his buddy Scott read, he might have learned about ways to change negative habits. Unfortunately for Brad, the small choices he made on a daily basis created a ripple that wreaked havoc on every area of his life.

Of course, all that calorie-counting and intellectual stimulation has had the opposite effect with Scott, who's now reaping the bounty of positive results. In *The Slight Edge*, Jeff Olson (another Jim Rohn protege) describes this as the repeating of simple daily disciplines versus the simple errors in judgement. It's that simple. With enough time and consistency, the outcomes become visible. Better yet, they're totally predictable.

The Compound Effect is predictable and measurable— that's great news! Isn't it comforting to know you only need to take a series of tiny steps, consistently, over time, to radically improve your life? Doesn't that sound easier than mustering up some grand show of bravery and heroic strength, only to wear yourself out and have to drum up all that energy again at a later date for another try (which will likely be unsuccessful)? I'm exhausted just thinking about it. But that's what people do. We've been conditioned by society to believe in the effectiveness of a great display of massive effort. Heck, it's downright all-American! See Figure 1.

Fig. 1

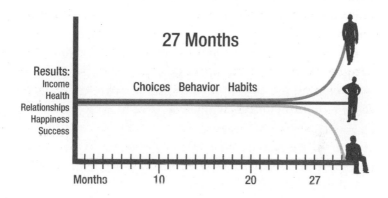

The beauty of the Compound Effect is in its simplicity. Notice how, on the left side of the diagram, the results are intangible, but how powerfully they differ later on. The behaviors all along the way are exactly the same, but the magic of the Compound Effect eventually kicks in to bring massive differences in results.

Success, Old School

The most challenging aspect of the Compound Effect is that we have to keep working away for a while, consistently and efficiently, before we can begin to see the payoff. Our grandparents knew this, though they didn't spend their evenings glued to the TV watching infomercials about how to have thin thighs in thirty days or a real estate kingdom in six months. I bet your grandparents worked six days a week, from sunup to sundown, using the skills they learned in their youth and repeatedly throughout their entire life. They knew the secret was hard work, discipline, and good habits.

It's interesting that wealth tends to skip a generation. Overwhelming abundance often leads to a lackadaisical mentality, which brings about a sedentary lifestyle. Children of the wealthy are especially susceptible. They weren't the ones who developed the discipline and character to create the wealth in the first place, so it makes sense that they may not have the same sense of value for wealth or understand what's necessary to keep it. We frequently see this entitlement mentality in children of royalty, movie stars, and corporate executives—and to a lesser degree, in children and adults everywhere.

As a nation, our entire populace seems to have lost appreciation for the value of a strong work ethic. We've had two, if not three, generations of Americans who have known great prosperity, wealth, and ease. Our expectations of what it really takes to create lasting success—things like grit, hard work, and fortitude—aren't alluring, and thus have been mostly forgotten. We've lost respect for the strife and struggle of our forefathers. The massive effort they put forth instilled discipline, chiseled their character, and stoked the spirit to brave new frontiers.

The truth is, complacency has impacted all great empires, including, but not limited to, the Egyptians, Greeks, Romans, Spanish, Portuguese, French, and English. Why? Because nothing fails like success. Once-dominant empires have failed for this very reason. People get to a certain level of success and get too comfortable.

Having experienced extended periods of prosperity, health, and wealth, we become complacent. We stop doing what we did to get us there. We become like the frog in the boiling water that doesn't jump to his freedom because the warming is so incremental and insidious that he doesn't notice he's getting cooked!

If we want to succeed, we need to recover our grandparents' work ethic.

It's time to restore our character, if not for the sake of saving America, at least for your own greater success and achievement. Don't buy into the genie in a lamp idea. You can sit on your couch waiting to attract checks in your mailbox, rub crystals together, walk on fire, channel that 2,000-year-old guru, or chant affirmations if you want to, but much of that is hocus-pocus commercialism manipulating you by appealing to your weaknesses. Real and lasting success requires work—and lots of it!

I have a quick, real-time story to illustrate this nothing-fails-like success concept: A great new restaurant opened up close to my home on the beach in San Diego. In the beginning, the place was always immaculate, the hostess had a big, welcoming smile for everyone, the service was impeccable (the manager came over and assured it), and the food was sensational. Soon, people started lining up to eat there and would often wait more than an hour to be seated.

Then, unfortunately, the restaurant's staff began to take its success for granted. The hostess became snooty, the service staff disheveled and curt, and the food quality hit-or-miss. The place was out of business within eighteen months. They failed because of their success. Or rather, because they stopped doing what made them successful to begin with. Their success clouded their perspective and they slacked off.

Microwave Mentality

Understanding the Compound Effect will rid you of "insta-results" expectation—the belief success should be as fast as your fast food, your one-hour glasses, your thirty-minute photo processing, your overnight mail, your microwave eggs, your instant hot water and text messaging. Enough, okay?

Promise yourself that you're going to let go once and for all of your lottery-winner expectations because, let's face it, you only hear stories about the *one* winner, not the millions of losers. That person you see jumping up and down in front of the Vegas slot machine or at the Santa Anita horse track doesn't reveal the hundreds of times that same person lost. If we go back to our mathematical chance of a positive result, again, we have a rounding error of zero—as in, you have about *zero* chance of winning. Harvard psychologist Daniel Gilbert, author of *Stumbling on Happiness*, says that if we gave lottery losers each thirty seconds on TV to announce not, "I won!" but "I lost," it would take almost nine years to get through the losers of a single drawing!

When you understand how the Compound Effect works, you won't pine for quick fixes or silver bullets. Don't try to fool yourself into believing that a mega-successful athlete didn't live through regular bone-crushing drills and thousands of hours of practice. He got up early to practice—and kept practicing long after all others had stopped. He faced the sheer agony and frustration of the failure, loneliness, hard work, and disappointment it took to become No. 1.

By the end of this book, or even before, I want you to know in your bones that your only path to success is through a continuum of mundane, unsexy, unexciting, and sometimes difficult daily disciplines compounded over time. Know, too, that the results, the life, and the lifestyle of your dreams can be yours when you put the Compound Effect to work for you. If you use the principles outlined in *The Compound Effect*, you will create your fairy-tale ending! See Figure 2.

Fig. 2

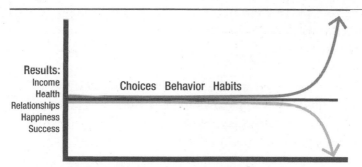

The Compound Effect is always working. You can choose to make it work for you, or you can ignore it and experience the negative effects of this powerful principle. It doesn't matter where you are on this graph. Starting today, you can decide to make simple, positive changes and allow the Compound Effect to take you where you want to go.

Have I made my point? Good. Join me in the next chapter, where we will focus on the one thing that controls your life. Every victory or defeat, triumph, or failure has started with this. Everything you have or don't have in your life right now has been because of this. Learn to change this, and you can change your life. Let's discover what this is…

Put the Compound Effect to Work for You

Summary Action Steps

↗ Write out a few excuses you might be clinging to (e.g., not smart enough, no experience, wrong upbringing, don't have the education, etc.). Decide to make up in hard work and personal development to outcompete anyone—including your old self.

↗ Be Scott—Write out the half-dozen small, seemingly inconsequential steps you can take every day that can take your life in a completely new and positive direction.

↗ Don't be Brad—Write down the small, seemingly inconsequential actions you can stop doing that might be compounding your results downward.

↗ List a few areas, skills, or outcomes where you have you been most successful in the past. Consider whether you could be taking those for granted and are not continuing to improve, and are therefore in jeopardy of having that complacency lead to future failure.

CHAPTER 2

CHOICES

We all come into this world the same: naked, scared, and ignorant. After that grand entrance, the life we end up with is simply an accumulation of all the choices we make. Our choices can be our best friend or our worst enemy. They can deliver us to our goals or send us orbiting into a galaxy far, far away.

Think about it. Everything in your life exists because you first made a *choice* about something. Choices are at the root of every one of your results. Each choice starts a behavior that over time becomes a habit. Choose poorly, and you just might find yourself back at the drawing board, forced to make new, often harder choices. Don't choose at all, and you've made the choice to be the passive receiver of whatever comes your way.

In essence, you make your choices, and then your choices make you. Every decision, no matter how slight, alters the trajectory of your life—whether or not to go to college, whom to marry, to have that last drink before you drive, to indulge in gossip or stay silent, to make one more prospecting call or call it a day, to say I love you or not. Every choice has an impact on the Compound Effect of your life.

This chapter is about becoming aware of and making choices that support the expansion of your life. Sounds complicated, but you'll be amazed by its simplicity. No longer will 99 percent of your choices be unconscious. No more will most of your daily routines and traditions come as a reaction to your programming. You'll ask yourself (and be able to answer), "How many of my behaviors have I not 'voted on'? What am I doing that I didn't consciously choose to do, yet continue to do every day?"

By employing the same idiot-proof strategies I've used to catapult my own life and career, strengthened by the Compound Effect, you'll be able to loosen the mysterious grip of the things that are unwinding your life and pulling you in the wrong direction. You'll be able to hit the Pause button before stumbling into idiot territory. You'll experience the ease of making decisions that lead to behaviors and habits that support you, every time.

Your biggest challenge isn't that you've intentionally been making bad choices. Heck, that would be easy to fix. Your biggest challenge is that you've been *sleepwalking* through your choices. Half the time, you're not even aware you're making them! Our choices are often shaped by our culture and upbringing. They can be so entwined in our routine behaviors and habits that they seem beyond our control. For instance, have you ever been going about your business, enjoying your life, when all of sudden you made a stupid choice or series of small choices that ultimately sabotaged your hard work and momentum, all for no apparent reason? You didn't intend to sabotage yourself, but by *not* thinking about your decisions—weighing the risks and potential outcomes—you found yourself facing unintended consequences. Nobody *intends* to become obese, go through bankruptcy, or get a divorce, but often (if not always) those consequences are the result of a series of small, poor choices.

Elephants Don't Bite

Have you ever been bitten by an elephant? How about a mosquito? It's the little things in life that will bite you. Occasionally, we see big mistakes threaten to destroy a career or reputation in an instant—the famous comedian who rants racial slurs during a stand-up routine, the drunken anti-Semitic antics of a once-celebrated humanitarian, the anti-gay-rights senator caught soliciting gay sex in a restroom, the admired female tennis player who uncharacteristically threatens an official with a tirade of expletives. Clearly, these types of poor choices have major repercussions. But even if you've pulled such a whopper in your past, it's not extraordinary massive steps backward or the tragic single moments that we're concerned with here.

For most of us, it's the frequent, small, and seemingly inconsequential choices that are of grave concern. I'm talking about the decisions you think don't make any difference at all. It's the little things that inevitably and predictably derail your success. Whether they're bone-headed maneuvers, no-biggie behaviors, or are disguised as positive choices (those are especially insidious), these seemingly insignificant decisions can completely throw you off course because you're not mindful of them. You get overwhelmed, space out, and are unaware of the little actions that take you way off course. The Compound Effect works, all right. It *always* works, remember? But in this case it works against you because you're doing... you're sleepwalking.

For instance, you inhale a soda and bag of potato chips and suddenly realize only after you polished off the last chip that you blew an entire day of healthy eating—and you weren't even hungry. You get caught up and lose two hours watching mindless TV—scratch that, let's give you some credit and make it an educational documentary—before realizing you spaced on preparing for an important presentation to land a valuable client. You blurt out a knee-jerk lie to a loved one for no good reason, when the truth would have worked just fine. What's going on?

You've allowed yourself to make a choice without thinking. And as long as you're making choices unconsciously, you can't consciously choose to change that ineffective behavior and turn it into productive habits. It's time to WAKE UP and make empowering choices.

Thanksgiving Year-Round

It's easy to point fingers at others, isn't it? "I'm not getting ahead because of my lame boss." "I would have gotten that promotion if it hadn't been for that backstabbing co-worker." "I'm always in a bad mood because my kids are driving me crazy." We're particularly gifted in the finger-pointing department when it comes to our romantic relationships—you know, where the *other* person is the one who needs to change.

A few years back, a friend of mine was complaining about his wife. From my observation, she was a terrific lady, and he was lucky to have her. I told him as much, but he continued to point out all the ways she was responsible for his unhappiness. That's when I shared an experience that had literally changed my marriage. One Thanksgiving, I decided to keep a Thanks Giving journal for my wife. Every day for an entire year I logged at least one thing I appreciated about her—the way she interacted with her friends, how she cared for our dogs, the fresh bed she prepared, a succulent meal she whipped up, or the beautiful way she styled her hair that day—whatever. I looked for the things my wife was doing that touched me, or revealed attributes, characteristics, or qualities I appreciated. I wrote them all down secretly for the entire year. By the end of that year, I'd filled an entire journal.

When I gave it to her the following Thanksgiving, she cried, calling it the best gift she'd ever received. (Even better than the BMW I'd given her for her birthday!) The funny thing was that the person most affected by this gift was me. All that journaling forced me to focus on my wife's positive aspects. I was consciously looking for all the things she was doing "right." That heartfelt focus overwhelmed anything I might have otherwise complained about. I fell deeply in love with her all over again (maybe even more than ever, as I was seeing subtleties in her nature and behavior instead of her more obvious qualities). My appreciation, gratitude, and intention to find the best in her was something I held in my heart and eyes each day. This caused me to show up differently in my marriage, which, of course, made her respond differently to me. Soon, I had even more things to write in my Thanks Giving journal! As a result of choosing to take a mere five minutes every day or so to document all the reasons why I was grateful for her, we experienced one of the best years of our marriage, and it's only gotten better.

After I shared my experience, my friend decided to keep a Thanks Giving journal about his wife. Within the first few months, he completely turned around his marriage. Choosing to look for and focus on his wife's positive qualities changed his view of her, which changed how he interacted with her. As a result, she made different choices about the way she responded to him. The cycle perpetuated. Or, shall we say, *compounded*.

Use the Gratitude Assessment sheet on page 166 to bolster your abundant mindset, or download at www.TheCompoundEffect.com/free

Owning 100 Percent

We are all self-made men and women, but only the successful take credit for it. I was eighteen when I was introduced to the idea of personal responsibility at a seminar, and the concept completely transformed my life. If you threw out the rest of this book and only practiced this one concept, within two to three years the changes in your life would be so great, your friends and family would have difficulty remembering the "old you."

In that seminar I attended at eighteen, the speaker asked, "What percentage of shared responsibility do you have in making a relationship work?" I was a teenager, so wise in the ways of true love. Of course I had all the answers.

"Fifty/fifty!" I blurted out. It was so obvious; both people must be willing to share the responsibility evenly or someone's getting ripped off.

"Fifty-one/forty-nine," yelled someone else, arguing that you'd have to be willing to do more than the other person. Aren't relationships built on self-sacrifice and generosity?

."Eighty/twenty," yelled another.

The instructor turned to the easel and wrote 100/0 on the paper in big black letters. "You have to be willing to give 100 percent with zero expectation of receiving anything in return," he said. "Only when you're willing to take 100 percent responsibility for making the relationship work will it work. Otherwise, a relationship left to chance will always be vulnerable to disaster."

Whoa. This wasn't what I was expecting! But I quickly understood how this concept could transform every area of my life. If I *always* took 100 percent responsibility for everything I experienced—completely owning all of my choices and all the ways I responded to whatever happened to me—I held the power. Everything was up to me. I was responsible for everything I did, didn't do, or how I responded to what was done to me.

I know you think you take responsibility for your life. I've yet to ask anybody who doesn't say, "Of *course*, I take responsibility for my life." But then you look at how most people operate in the world; there's a lot of finger pointing, victimhood, blaming, and expecting someone else or the government to solve their problems. If you've ever blamed traffic for being late, or decided you are in a bad mood because of something your kid, spouse, or co-worker did, you're not taking 100 percent personal responsibility. You arrived late because the printer was busy? Maybe you shouldn't have waited until the last minute? Co-worker messed up the presentation? Shouldn't you have double-checked it yourself before delivering it? Not getting along with your unreasonable teen? There are a countless fantastic books and classes to help you learn how to deal.

You alone are responsible for what you *do, don't do,* or how you *respond* to what's done to you. This empowering mindset revolutionized my life. Luck, circumstances, or the right situation wasn't what mattered. If *it* was to be, *it* was up to me. I was free to fly. No matter who was elected president, how badly the economy tanked, or what anybody said, did, or didn't do, I was still 100 percent in control of *me.* Through choosing to be officially liberated from past, present, and future victimhood, I'd hit the jackpot. I had the unlimited power to control my destiny.

Getting Lucky

Maybe you believe you're simply unlucky. But really, that's just another excuse. The difference between becoming fabulously rich, happy, and healthy, or broke, depressed, and unhealthy, is the choices you make throughout life. Nothing else will make the difference. Here's the thing about luck: We're all lucky. If you are on the right side of the dirt, have your health, and a little food in your cupboard, you are incredibly lucky. Everyone has the opportunity to be "lucky," because beyond having the basics of health and sustenance, luck simply comes down to a series of choices.

When I asked Richard Branson if he felt luck played a part in his success, he answered, "Yes, of course, we are all lucky. If you live in a free society, you are lucky. Luck surrounds us every day; we are constantly having lucky things happen to us, whether you recognize it or not. I have not been any more lucky or unlucky than anyone else. The difference is when luck came my way, I took advantage of it."

Ah, spoken like a man knighted with wisdom. While we're on the topic, it's my belief that the old adage we often hear— "Luck is when opportunity meets preparation"—isn't enough. I believe there are two other critical components to "luck."

The (Complete) Formula for Getting Lucky:
Preparation (personal growth) +
Attitude (belief/mindset) +
Opportunity (a good thing coming your way) +
Action (doing something about it) =
Luck

Preparation: By consistently improving and preparing yourself—your skills, knowledge, expertise, relationships, and resources—you have the wherewithal to take advantage of great opportunities when they arise (when luck "strikes"). Then, you can be like Arnold Palmer, who told *SUCCESS* magazine in February of 2009, "It's a funny thing; the more I practice, the luckier I get."

Attitude: This is where luck evades most people, and where Sir Richard is spot-on with his belief that luck is all around us. It's simply a matter of seeing situations, conversations, and circumstances as fortuitous. You cannot see what you don't look for, and you cannot look for what you don't believe in.

Opportunity: It's possible to make your own luck, but the luck I'm talking about here isn't planned for, or it comes faster or differently than expected. In this stage of the formula, luck isn't forced. It's a natural occurrence, and it often shows up seemingly of its own accord.

Action: This is where you come in. However this luck was delivered to you—from the universe, God, the Lucky Charms leprechaun, or whomever or whatever you associate delivering your good fortune—it's now your job to act on it. This is what separates the Richard Bransons from the Joseph Wallingtons. Joseph who? Exactly. You've never heard of him. That's because he failed to take action on all the lucky things that happened to him.

So no more whining about the cards you were dealt, the great defeats you suffered, or any other circumstances. Countless people have more disadvantages and greater obstacles than you, and yet they're wealthier and more fulfilled. Luck is an equal-opportunity distributor. Lady luck shines on all, but rather than having your umbrella overhead, you've got to have your face to the sky. When it comes down to it, it's all you, baby. There's no other way around it.

The High Price of Tuition at UHK (University of Hard Knocks)

Nearly a decade ago I was asked to be a partner in a new startup venture. I invested a considerable sum of money into the deal and worked tirelessly on it for nearly two years before finding out that my partner had mismanaged and squandered all the cash. I lost more than $330,000. I didn't try to sue him; in fact, I lent him more money later for a personal situation. The bottom line was the loss was my fault. I had agreed to be his partner without doing enough due diligence on his background and personal character. During our time in business, I wasn't inspecting what I was expecting. I could justify it by saying I trusted him, but the truth was I was guilty of being lazy by not watching the finances more diligently. Not only had I made the choice to start this relationship and business, but I'd also made many choices to ignore obvious red flags and warning signs. Because I chose to not be completely responsible for the business, in the end, I was responsible for the results. When I learned of the wrongdoings, I chose not to lose any more time fighting it. Instead, I licked my wounds, learned my lesson, and moved on. In hindsight, I'd make the same choice to pick up and move on again today.

I now challenge you to do the same. No matter what has happened to you, take complete responsibility for it—good or bad, victory or defeat. Own it. My mentor Jim Rohn said, "The day you graduate from childhood to adulthood is the day you take full responsibility for your life."

Today is graduation day! From this day forward, choose to be 100 percent responsible for your life. Eliminate all of your excuses. Embrace the fact that you are freed by your choices, as long as you assume personal responsibility for them.

It's time to make the choice to take control.

Your Secret Weapon—Your Scorecard

I'm about to walk you through one of the single greatest strategies I've ever used in my personal development. This strategy helps me take control of the choices I make throughout the day, causing *everything* else to fall into place, and leading to behaviors and actions that shepherd my habits into line like dutiful, loyal minions.

Right this moment: Pick an area of your life where you most want to be successful. Do you want more money in the bank? A trimmer waistline? The strength to compete in an Iron Man event? A better relationship with your spouse or kids? Picture where you are in that area, right now. Now picture where you want to be: richer, thinner, happier, you name it. The first step toward change is awareness. If you want to get from where you are to where you want to be, you have to start by becoming aware of the choices that lead you away from your desired destination. Become very conscious of every choice you make today so you can begin to make smarter choices moving forward.

To help you become aware of your choices, I want you to *track every action* that relates to the area of your life you want to improve. If you've decided you want get out of debt, you're going to track every penny you pull from your pocket. If you've decided you want to lose weight, you're going to track everything you put into your mouth. If you've decided to train for an athletic event, you're going to track every step you take, every workout you do. Simply carry around a small notebook, something you'll keep in your pocket or purse at all times, and a writing instrument. You're going to write it all down. Every day. Without fail. No excuses, no exceptions. As if Big Brother's watching you. As if my dad and I will come and make you do a hundred pushups every time you miss.

Doesn't sound like much, I know—writing things down on a little piece of paper. But tracking *my* progress and missteps is the one of the reasons I've accumulated the success I have. The process forces you to be conscious of your decisions. But as Jim Rohn would say, "What's simple to do is also simple not to do." The magic is not in the complexity of the task; the magic is in the doing of simple things repeatedly and long enough to ignite the miracle of the Compound Effect. So, beware of neglecting the simple things that make the big things in your life possible. The biggest difference between successful people and unsuccessful people is that successful people are willing to do what unsuccessful people are not. Remember that; it will come in handy many times throughout life when faced with a difficult, tedious, or tough choice.

Money Trap

I learned the power of tracking the hard way, after I'd acted like a colossal idiot about my finances. Back in my early twenties, when I was making a lot of money selling real estate, I met with my accountant.

"You owe well over $100,000 in taxes," he said.

"What?!" I said. "I don't have that kind of cash just lying around."

"Why not?" he asked. "You collected several times that; certainly you set aside the taxes that would be due on that money."

"Evidently I didn't," I said.

"Where did the money go?" he asked.

"I don't know," I said, a sobering confession, for sure. The money had passed through my hands like water, and I hadn't even noticed!

Then my accountant did me a great favor.

"Son," he said, looking me dead in the eyes, "you've got to get a grip. I've seen this a hundred times before. You're spending money like a drunken fool, and you don't even know how to account for it. That's stupid. Stop it. You are now seriously in the hole. You have to earn more money that you'll owe additional taxes on just to pay for your back taxes. Continue this, and you'll dig your financial grave with your own wallet."

I immediately got the message.

Here's what my accountant had me do: carry a small notepad in my back pocket, and write down every single cent I spent for thirty days. Whether it was a thousand dollars for a new suit or fifty cents for air to fill up my tires, it all had to go down on the notepad. Wow. This brought an instantaneous awareness of the many unconscious choices I was making that resulted in money pouring out of my pockets. Because I had to log everything, I resisted buying some things, just so I didn't have to take out the notepad and write it in the dang book!

Keeping a money log for thirty days straight cemented a new awareness in me, and created a completely new set of choices and disciplines around my spending. And, since awareness and positive behaviors compound, I found myself being more proactive with money in general, putting away more for retirement, finding areas to save where there was clear waste, and enjoying the fun quotient of money—"play money"—all the more. When I did consider shelling out for entertainment, I did so only after a *long* pause.

This tracking exercise changed my awareness of how I related to my money. It worked so well, in fact, that I've used it many times to change other behaviors. Tracking is my go-to transformation model for everything that ails me. Over the years I've tracked what I eat and drink, how much I exercise, how much time I spend improving a skill, my number of sales calls, even the improvement of my relationships with family, friends, or my spouse. The results have been no less profound than my money-tracking wake-up call.

In buying this book, you're basically paying me for my opinion, my guidance. This is where I'm going to become a hard-ass and insist you track your behaviors for at least one whole week. This book isn't designed to entertain you; it is designed to help you get results. To get results, you have to take some action.

You may have heard about tracking before. In fact, you've probably done your own version of this exercise. But I also bet you aren't doing it now, right? How do I know? *Because your life isn't working as successfully as you'd like.* You've gotten derailed. Tracking is the way to get it back on track.

Do you know how the casinos make so much money in Vegas? Because they track every table, every winner, every hour. Why do Olympic trainers get paid top dollar? Because they track every workout, every calorie, and every micronutrient for their athletes. All winners are trackers. Right now I want you to track your life with the same intention: to bring your goals within sight.

Tracking is a simple exercise. It works because it brings moment-to-moment awareness to the actions you take in the area of your life you want to improve. You'll be surprised at what you will observe about your behavior. You cannot manage or improve something until you measure it. Likewise, you can't make the most of who you are—your talents and resources and capabilities—until you are aware of and accountable for your actions. Every professional athlete and his or her coach track each performance down to the smallest minutiae. Pitchers know their stats on every pitch in their repertoire. Golfers have even more metrics on their swings. Professional athletes know how to adjust their performances based on what they've tracked. They pay attention to what they record and make changes accordingly, because they know when their stats improve they win more games and earn more in endorsement deals.

At any given moment, I want you to know exactly how well you're doing. I'm asking you to track yourself as if you're a valuable commodity. Because you are. Want that idiot-proof system we talked about earlier? This is it. So, regardless of whether you think you're aware of your habits or not (believe me, you're not!), I'm asking you to start tracking. Doing so will revolutionize your life, and ultimately, your lifestyle.

Keep It Slow and Easy

Don't panic. We're starting off with an easy, breezy tempo. Just track *one* habit for *one* week. Pick the habit that has the greatest control over you; that's where you'll start. Once you begin reaping the rewards of the Compound Effect, you'll naturally *want* to introduce this practice into other areas of your life. In other words, you'll *choose* to choose tracking.

Let's say the category you choose is getting your eating under control because you want to lose weight. Your task is to write down everything you put in your mouth, from the steak, potatoes, and salad you have at dinner, to those many tiny choices during the day—that handful of pretzels in the break room, that second slice of cheese on your sandwich, that "fun-sized" candy bar, that sample at Costco, those extra sips of wine after the host tops off your glass. Don't forget the beverages. They all add up, but unless tracked, they're easy to dismiss or forget because they seem so small. Again, merely writing these things down sounds simple—and it *is*—BUT ONLY WHEN YOU DO IT. That's why I'm asking that you commit to choosing a category and a start date, now, *before you turn this page.*

I am going to start tracking _____ **on** _____.
[date/month/year]

What will the tracking look like? It will be thorough, as in organized. And relentless, as in constant. Each day you'll start with the date at the top of a fresh page, and start keeping track.

What happens after the first week of tracking? You'll probably be in shock. You'll be astonished at how those calories, pennies, minutes have been escaping you. You never even knew that they were there, let alone that they'd vanished.

Now, keep going. You're going to track in this one area for *three weeks.* Maybe you're already groaning; you just don't want to do it. But trust me: You'll be so blown away by the results after one week you'll sign yourself up for another two. I can practically guarantee it.

Why three weeks? You've heard psychologists say that something doesn't become a habit until you practice it for three weeks. It's not an exact science, but it's a good benchmark, and it has worked for me. So, ideally, I want you to stick with your choice to track your behaviors for twenty-one days. If you refuse, I'm not going to lose anything (heck, it's not my waistline, cardiovascular health, bank balance, or relationship you're messing with!). But, seriously, you're reading this book because you want to change your life, right? And I promised you it was going to take slow, steady work, didn't I? This one action isn't easy, but it's simple and doable. So do it.

Promise yourself to start. Today. For the next three weeks, choose to carry around your own small notepad (or large one, if that's more enticing), and write *every single thing down in your category.*

What happens in three weeks? You move from the shock that follows the first week to the happy surprise of seeing how merely becoming conscious of your actions begins to shape them. You'll find yourself asking, "Do I really want that candy bar? I'm gonna have to haul out my notebook and write it down, and I'll feel a little sheepish." That's two hundred calories saved right there. Turn down that candy bar every day, and in a little more than two weeks, you'll have already lost a pound! You'll start adding up that $4.00 coffee on the way to work and realize, *Holy cow! I've just spent sixty bucks on coffee in three weeks!* Hey, that's a thousand bucks a year! Or, compounded, that's $51,833.79 in twenty years! How much do you *really* need to stop for coffee? See Figure 3.

Fig. 3

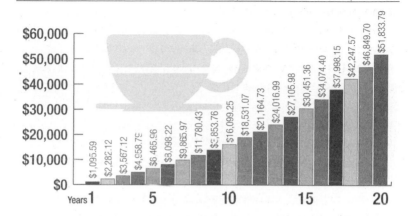

The real cost of a four-dollar-a-day coffee habit over 20 years is
$51,833.79. That's the power of the Compound Effect.

Come again? Am I saying that your four-dollar-a-day
coffee habit is going to cost you $51,833.79 in twenty years?
Yes, I am. Did you know that every dollar you spend today, no
matter where you spend it, is costing you nearly five dollars
in only twenty years (and ten dollars in thirty years)? That's
because if you took a dollar and invested it at 8 percent, in
twenty years, that dollar would be worth almost five. Every
time you spend a buck today, it's like taking five dollars out of
your future pocket.

I used to make the mistake of looking at a price tag and
thinking that if an item was listed at fifty dollars, it cost me
fifty dollars. Well, yes, in today's dollars. But if you consider
the potential value of that same fifty dollars after it has
been invested for twenty years the cost (what you lose by

spending that money rather than investing it) is four or five times greater! In other words, every time you look at an item that costs fifty dollars you have to ask, "Is this item worth $250?" If it's worth $250 to you today, then it's worth buying." Keep that in mind next time you go to a place like Costco, with all sorts of amazing things that you didn't know you had to have. You go in to buy twenty-five dollars' worth of necessities and walk out with $400 of stuff instead. My garage looks like a Costco graveyard. Next time you walk into one of those bargain basement stores, assess things from this future-value standpoint. Chances are you'll put down that fifty-dollar crepe maker so Future You will have $250 more in the bank. Make the correct choice every day, every week for many years, and you can quickly see how you can become financially abundant.

When you track with this awareness, you'll find yourself showing up in your life very differently. You'll be able to ask yourself, "Is having a coffee once every workday worth the eventual price of a Mercedes-Benz?" Because that's what it's costing you. Even more than that, you're not sleepwalking anymore. You're aware and conscious and making better choices. All from a little notebook and pen. Simply amazing, isn't it?

The Unsung, Unseen Hero

Once you start tracking your life, your attention will be focused on the smallest things you're doing right, as well as the smallest things you're doing wrong. And when you choose to make even the smallest course corrections consistently, over time, you'll begin to see amazing results. But don't expect immediate fanfare. When I say "small" course corrections, I'm talking truly invisible. Chances are no one's going to notice them anytime soon. There will be no applause. No one's going to send you a congratulations card or a trophy for these disciplines. And yet, eventually, their compounding effect will result in an exceptional payoff. It's the littlest disciplines that pay off over time, the effort and preparation for the great triumph that happened when no one was looking. And yet the results are exceptional. A horse wins by a nose, but gets 10 times the prize money. Is the horse 10 times faster? No, just a little bit better. But it was those extra laps around the track, the extra discipline in the horse's nutrition, or the extra work by the jockey that made the results a slight bit better with compounded rewards.

After hundreds of tournaments played and thousands of strokes tallied, the difference between the No. 1 ranked golfer and the No. 10 golfer is an average of only 1.9 strokes, but the difference in prize money is five times (over $10 million versus $2 million)! The No. 1 golfer isn't five times better, not even 50 percent or even 10 percent better. In fact, the difference between his average score is only 2.7 percent better. Yet, the results are five times greater! See Figure 4.

Fig. 4

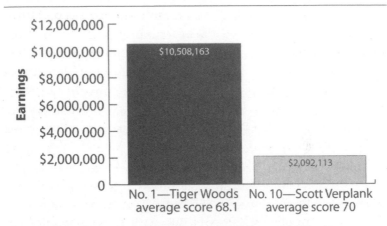

The difference between the No. 1 ranked golfer and the No. 10 golfer is an average of only 1.9 strokes, but the difference in prize money is five times. That's the power of the Compound Effect.

[Source: FedEx Cup Ranking as of mid-December 2009]

That's the power of little things adding up. It's not the big things that add up in the end; it's the hundreds, thousands, or millions of little things that separate the ordinary from the extraordinary. To be one stroke better requires countless little things that don't get accounted for when you're putting on the green jacket.

Let me give you a few more ways tracking small changes can result in huge payoffs.

Take a Walk

I was mentoring a CEO of a sizeable company doing more than $100 million in sales annually. Phil was an entrepreneur and founder of the company. The company was doing fine, but I detected a lack of engagement, trust, and enthusiasm in the culture of his organization. I wasn't too surprised; it turns out that Phil hadn't been in parts of his own building for more than five years! He'd never spoken personally to more than 80 percent of his staff! He basically lived in a bubble with his management team. I asked Phil to track just one change: three times a week, he had to step outside of his office and walk around the building. His goal was to seek out at least three people whom he saw doing things right or had heard good things about and give them some personal acknowledgment of his appreciation. This one small change in his behavior took less than an hour a week, but had massive effects over time. The employees Phil took the time to recognize began to go the extra mile and work harder to earn his greater appreciation. Other employees started to perform better, observing that great effort was recognized and appreciated. The ripple effect of their new attitude transferred to their customer interactions, improving the customers' experience with the company, increasing repeat and referral business, which increased everyone's pride. That simple change over the period of eighteen months did a complete 180 on the company culture. Net profits grew by more than 30 percent during that time, utilizing the same staff and zero additional investment in marketing. All because Phil committed to one small, seemingly insignificant step done consistently over time.

Money Tree

Twelve years ago I had a wonderful assistant, Kathleen. She earned $40,000 a year at the time. She was tasked to manage the registration table situated at the back of the room during one of my lectures on entrepreneurship and wealth building. The next week she came into my office. "I heard you talk about saving 10 percent of everything you earn," she told me. "That sounds nice, but there is no way I could do that. It's totally unrealistic!" She proceeded to tell me about all her bills and financial obligations. After she wrote them all out, it was obvious there really wasn't any money left over at the end of the month. "I need a raise," she said.

"I'll do better than that," I told her. "I'm going to teach you how to become wealthy." It wasn't the answer she was looking for, but she agreed.

I taught Kathleen how to track her spending, and she began to carry her notebook. I told her to open a separate savings account with only $33—just 1 percent of her existing monthly income. I then showed her how to live on $33 less the next month—bring in her own lunch just one day a week instead of going downstairs to the deli and ordering a sandwich, chips, and a drink. The next month I had her save only 2 percent ($67). She saved the additional $33 by changing her cable subscription service. The next month we went up to 3 percent. We canceled her subscription to *People* magazine (it was time to study *her own* life), and instead of going to Starbucks twice a week, I told Kathleen to buy the Starbucks beans and other fancy fixings and make her own coffee in the office (she grew to like that even better—me too!).

By the end of the year, Kathleen was saving 10 percent of every dollar she earned without noticing a significant impact on her lifestyle. She was amazed! That one discipline also had a ripple effect on many other disciplines in her life. She calculated what she spent on mind-numbing entertainment and began investing that money on personal growth instead. After feeding her mind with several hundred hours of inspirational and instructional content, her creativity started to soar. She brought me several ideas on how we could make and save more money in our organization. She presented me with a plan that she would implement in her spare time, if I promised to reward her with 10 percent of all the money saving strategies and 15 percent of all the new revenue strategies that proved profitable. By the end of the second year, she was earning more than $100,000 a year—on the same $40,000 base salary. Kathleen eventually started her own independent contract service business that took off. I ran into Kathleen at an airport two years ago. She now earns more than a quarter of a million dollars a year and has saved and created more than $1 million in assets—she's a millionaire! All starting from the choice to take one small step and start saving $33 a month!

Time Is of the Essence

The earlier you start making small changes, the more powerfully the Compound Effect works in your favor. Suppose your friend listened to Dave Ramsey's advice and began putting $250 a month into an IRA when she got her first job after graduating from college at age twenty-three. You, on the other hand, don't start saving until you're forty. (Or maybe you started saving a little earlier but cleaned out your retirement account because you didn't notice any great gains.) By the time your friend is forty, she never has to invest another dollar and will have more than a $1 million by the age of sixty-seven, growing at 8 percent interest compounded

Fig. 5

THE POWER OF THE COMPOUND EFFECT						
FRIEND			YOU			
Age	Year	Year-end Balance	Age	Year		
23	1	$3,112.48	23	1	0	
24	2	$6,483.30	24	2	0	
25	3	$10,133.89	25	3	0	
26	4	$14,087.48	26	4	0	
27	5	$18,369.21	27	5	0	
28	6	$23,006.33	28	6	0	
29	7	$28,028.33	29	7	0	
30	8	$33,467.15	30	8	0	
31	9	$39,357.38	31	9	0	
32	10	$45,736.51	32	10	0	
33	11	$52,645.10	33	11	0	
34	12	$60,127.10	34	12	0	
35	13	$68,230.10	35	13	0	
36	14	$77,005.64	36	14	0	
37	15	$86,509.56	37	15	0	
38	16	$96,802.29	38	16	0	
39	17	$107,949.31	39	17	0	
40	18	$120,021.53	40	18	0	
41	19	$129,983.26	41	19	$3,112.48	
42	20	$140,771.81	42	20	$6,483.30	
43	21	$152,455.80	43	21	$10,133.89	
44	22	$165,109.55	44	22	$14,087.48	
45	23	$178,813.56	45	23	$18,369.21	
46	24	$193,655.00	46	24	$23,006.33	
47	25	$209,728.27	47	25	$28,028.33	
48	26	$227,135.61	48	26	$33,467.15	
49	27	$245,987.76	49	27	$39,357.38	
50	28	$266,404.62	50	28	$45,736.51	
51	29	$288,516.07	51	29	$52,645.10	
52	30	$312,462.77	52	30	$60,127.10	
53	31	$338,397.02	53	31	$68,230.10	
54	32	$366,483.81	54	32	$77,005.64	
55	33	$396,901.78	55	33	$86,509.56	
56	34	$429,844.43	56	34	$96,802.29	
57	35	$465,521.31	57	35	$107,949.31	
58	36	$504,159.35	58	36	$120,021.53	
59	37	$546,004.33	59	37	$133,095.74	
60	38	$591,322.42	60	38	$147,255.10	
61	39	$640,401.89	61	39	$162,589.69	
62	40	$693,554.93	62	40	$179,197.03	
63	41	$751,119.64	63	41	$197,182.78	
64	42	$813,462.20	64	42	$216,661.33	
65	43	$880,979.16	65	43	$237,756.60	
66	44	$954,100.00	66	44	$260,602.76	
Total accumulated= 67	45	$1,033,289.83	67	45	$285,345.14	
Total amount invested=		$54,000.00			$81,000.00	

FRIEND

YOU

monthly. You continue to invest $250 every month until you reach sixty-seven, the normal retirement age for Social Security for those born after 1960. (That means you're saving for twenty-seven years in contrast to her seventeen years.) When you're ready to retire, you'll have less than $300,000 and will have invested $27,000 more than your friend. Even though you saved for many more years and invested much more cash, you still ended up with less than a third of the money you could have had. That's what happens when we procrastinate and neglect necessary behaviors, habits, and disciplines. Don't wait another day to start the small disciplines that will lead you in the direction of your goals! See Figure 5.

Are you telling yourself that you're starting so late that you're already way behind the eight ball and can never catch up? That's just another tired tape in your head; it's time to turn it off. It's never too late to reap the benefits of the Compound Effect. Suppose you've always wanted to play the piano, but feel it's too late because you're about to turn forty. If you start now, by the time you're retirement age, you could be a master, as you'll have been playing for twenty-five years! The key is to start NOW. Every great act, every fantastic adventure, starts with small steps. The first step always looks harder than it actually is.

But what if twenty-five years is too long? What if you've only got time or patience for ten years? In Brian Tracy's book *Focal Point* (Amacom, 2002), he models how to improve any area of your life by 1,000 percent. Not 10 percent or even 100 percent, but 1,000 percent! Let me outline it for you.

All you have to do is improve yourself, your performance, and your output and earnings by 1/10 of 1 percent each workday (you even get to slack off on weekends). That is 1/1,000. Do you think you could do that? Of course, anyone could do that. Simple. Do it each day of the week, and you'll improve by ½ percent each week (translation: not much), equaling 2 percent each month, which, compounded, adds up to 26 percent each year. Your income now doubles each 2.9 years. By Year Ten, you can be performing and earning 1,000 percent what you are now. Isn't that amazing? You don't have to put in 1,000 percent more effort or work 1,000 percent more hours. Just 1/10 of 1 percent improvement each day. That's it.

Success Is a (Half-) Marathon

Beverly was a salesperson for an educational software company for which I was doing a turnaround. One day she told me about her friend who was running a half-marathon the upcoming weekend. "I could *never* do such a thing," Beverly, who was significantly overweight, assured me. "I get winded going up a single flight of stairs!"

"If you want to, you can choose to do what your friend is doing," I told her. She balked, saying, "There's absolutely no way."

My first step was to help Beverly find her motivation. "So, Beverly, why would you want to run the half-marathon?"

"Well, my twenty-year high-school reunion is coming up next summer, and I want to look fabulous. But I've gained so much weight since I had my second child five years ago. I don't know how I can do it."

Bingo! Now we had a motivating goal. But I proceeded with caution. If you've ever tried to lose weight, you probably know the drill: Buy an expensive gym membership, drop a fortune on personal trainers, new equipment, spiffy new workout clothes, and great athletic footwear. Work out vigorously for a week or so and then turn your elliptical machine into a clothes-drying rack, ditch the gym, and let your sneakers mold in the corner. I wanted to try a better way with Beverly. I knew that if I could get her to choose just *one* new habit, she'd get hooked, and all the other behaviors would naturally fall into line.

I asked Beverly to drive her car around the block and map out a one-mile loop from her house. Then, I told her to walk the loop three times over a period of two weeks. Notice that I didn't ask her to start by running the mile. Instead, I started with something—a small, easy task that required no major stretch. Then I had her walk the loop three times in one week for an additional two weeks. Each day she made the choice to continue on.

Next I told Beverly to start a slow jog, only as far as she felt comfortable. As soon as she started feeling breathless, she was to stop and continue walking. I asked her to do this until she could run one-fourth, then one-half, and then three-quarters of that mile. It took three more weeks—nine outings—before she could jog a full mile. After a total of seven weeks, she was jogging the whole loop. That might seem like a long time for such a short victory, right? After all, half of a marathon is 13.1 miles. One mile is nothing. What was something, however, was that Beverly was beginning to see how her choice to get fit for the reunion—her why-power (as I'll soon explain)—was fueling her new health habits. The Compound Effect had been set in motion and was starting its miraculous process.

I then asked Beverly to increase her distance an eighth of a mile each outing (an almost unnoticeable length, maybe only 300 steps further). Within six months, she was running *nine* miles without any discomfort at all. In nine months, she was running 13.5 miles regularly (more than the distance of a half-marathon) as part of her running routine. More exciting, though, was what happened in other areas of her life. Beverly lost her cravings for chocolate (a lifelong obsession) and heavy, fatty foods. Gone. The increased energy she felt from the cardiovascular exercise and better eating choices helped her bring more enthusiasm to her work. Her sales performance doubled during the same period (which was great for me!).

As we saw in the previous chapter, the ripple effects of all this momentum raised her self-esteem which made her more affectionate toward her husband. Their relationship became more passionate than it had been since college. Because she had renewed energy, her interaction with her children became more active and animated. She noticed she no longer had time to hang out with her "Debbie Downer" friends, who still gathered together after work for greasy appetizers and drinks. She made new "healthy" friends in a running club she joined—which led to a whole host of additional positive choices, behaviors, and habits.

Following that first conversation in my office and Beverly's decision to find her why-power and commit to a series of small steps, she lost more than forty pounds, becoming a walking (and running) billboard for fit and empowered women. Today, Beverly runs full marathons!

Your life is the product of your moment-to-moment choices. In our *SUCCESS* CD (May 2010), TV's *Biggest Loser* fitness trainer Jillian Michaels shared with me a powerful childhood story: "When I was a kid, my mom would have these elaborate Easter egg hunts for me. I would run around the house, and when I would get close to a hidden egg, she'd say, 'Oh you're warm.' You know, you get closer to it, 'Oh, you're on fire.' And then you move away from the egg and she'd go, 'Oh, you're cold, you're freezing.' I teach contestants that, on a moment-to-moment basis, I need them to think about their happiness and their ultimate goal as being warm—how every choice and every decision they make in the moment is getting them closer to that ultimate goal."

Since your outcomes are all a result of your moment-to-moment choices, you have incredible power to change your life by changing those choices. Step by step, day by day, your choices will shape your actions until they become habits, where practice makes them permanent.

Losing is a habit. So is winning. Now let's work on permanently instilling winning habits into your life. Eliminate sabotaging habits and instill the needed positive habits, and you can take your life in any direction you desire, to the heights of your greatest imagination. Let me show you how…

Put the Compound Effect to Work for You

Summary Action Steps

↗ What area, person, or circumstance in your life do you struggle with the most? Start journaling all the aspects of that situation that you are grateful for. Keep a record of everything that reinforces and expands your gratitude in that area.

↗ Where in your life are you not taking 100 percent responsibility for the success or failure of your present condition? Write down three things you have done in the past that have messed things up. List three things you should have done but didn't. Write out three things that happened to you but you responded poorly. Write down three things you can start doing right now to take back responsibility for the outcomes of your life.

↗ Start tracking at least one behavior in one area of your life you'd like to change and improve (e.g., money, nutrition, fitness, recognizing others, parenting... any area).

CHAPTER 3

HABITS

A wise teacher was taking a stroll through the forest with a young pupil and stopped before a tiny tree.

"Pull up that sapling," the teacher instructed his pupil, pointing to a sprout just coming up from the earth. The youngster pulled it up easily with his fingers. "Now pull up that one," said the teacher, indicating a more established sapling that had grown to about knee high to the boy. With little effort, the lad yanked and the tree came up, roots and all. "And now, this one," said the teacher, nodding toward a more well-developed evergreen that was as tall as the young pupil. With great effort, throwing all his weight and strength into the task, using sticks and stone he found to pry up the stubborn roots, the boy finally got the tree loose.

"Now," the wise one said, "I'd like you to pull this one up." The young boy followed the teacher's gaze, which fell upon a mighty oak so tall the boy could scarcely see the top. Knowing the great struggle he'd just had pulling up the much smaller tree, he simply told his teacher, "I am sorry, but I can't."

"My son, you have just demonstrated the power that habits will have over your life!" the teacher exclaimed. "The older they are, the bigger they get, the deeper the roots grow, and the harder they are to uproot. Some get so big, with roots so deep, you might hesitate to even try."

Creatures of Habit

Aristotle wrote, "We are what we repeatedly do." Merriam-Webster defines habit this way: "An acquired mode of behavior that has become nearly or completely involuntary."

There's a story about a man riding a horse, galloping quickly. It appears that he's going somewhere very important. A man standing along the roadside shouts, "Where are you going?" The rider replies, "I don't know. Ask the horse!" This is the story of most people's lives; they're riding the horse of their habits, with no idea where they're headed. It's time to take control of the reins, and move your life in the direction of where you really want to go.

If you've been living on autopilot and allowing your habits to run you, I want you to understand why. And I want you to let yourself off the hook. After all, you're in good company. Psychological studies reveal that 95 percent of everything we feel, think, do, and achieve is a result of a learned habit! We're born with instincts, of course, but no habits at all. We develop them over time. Beginning in childhood, we learned a series of conditioned responses that led us to react automatically (as in, without thinking) to most situations.

In your day-to-day life, living "automatically" has its definite positives. If you had to consciously think about every step of each ordinary task—making breakfast, driving the kids to school, getting to work, and so on—your life would grind to a halt. You probably brush your teeth twice a day on autopilot. There's no big philosophical debate; you just do it. You strap on your seatbelt the minute your butt hits the seat. No second thoughts. Our habits and routines allow us to use minimal conscious energy for everyday tasks. They help keep us sane and enable us to handle most situations reasonably well. And because we don't have to think about the mundane, we can focus our mental energy on more creative and enriching thoughts. Habits can be helpful—as long as they're good habits, that is.

If you eat healthfully, you've likely built healthy habits around the food you buy and what you order at restaurants. If you're fit, it's probably because you work out regularly. If you're successful in a sales job, it's probably because your habits of mental preparation and positive self-talk enable you to stay optimistic in the face of rejection.

I've met and worked with many great achievers, CEOs, and "superstars," and I can tell you they *all* share one common trait—they all have good habits. That's not to say they don't have bad habits; they do. But not many. A daily routine built on good habits is the difference that separates the most successful amongst us from everyone else. And doesn't that make sense? From what we've already discussed, you know successful people aren't necessarily more intelligent or more talented than anyone else. But their habits take them in the direction of becoming more informed, more knowledgeable, more competent, better skilled, and better prepared.

My dad used Larry Bird as an example to teach me about habits when I was a kid. "Larry Legend" is known as one of the greatest professional basketball players. But he wasn't known for being the most athletically talented player. Nobody would have described Larry as "graceful" on the basketball court. Yet, despite his limited natural athletic ability, he led the Boston Celtics to three world championships and remains one of the best players of all time. How did he do it?

It was Larry's habits—his relentless dedication to practice and to improve his game. Bird was one of the most consistent free-throw shooters in the history of the NBA. Growing up, his habit was to practice five hundred free-throw shots every morning before school. With that kind of discipline, Larry made the most of his God-given talents and kicked the butts of some of the most "gifted" players on the court.

Like Larry Bird, you can condition your automatic and unconscious responses to be those of a developed champion. This chapter is about choosing to make up for what you lack in innate ability with discipline, hard work, and good habits. It's about becoming a creature of champion habits.

With enough practice and repetition, any behavior, good or bad, becomes automatic over time. That means that even though we developed most of our habits unconsciously (by modeling our parents, responding to environmental or cultural associations, or creating coping mechanisms), we can consciously decide to change them. It stands to reason that since you learned every habit you have, you can also unlearn the ones that aren't serving you well. Ready? Here goes...

Start by Thinking Your Way Out of the Instant Gratification Trap

We understand that scarfing Pop-Tarts won't slenderize our waistlines. We realize that logging three hours a night watching *Dancing with the Stars* and *NCIS* leaves us with three fewer hours to read a good book or listen to a terrific audio. We "get" that merely purchasing great running shoes doesn't make us marathon-ready. We're a "rational" species—at least that's what we tell ourselves. So why are we so irrationally enslaved by so many bad habits? It's because our need for immediate gratification can turn us into the most reactive, nonthinking animals around.

If you took a bite of a Big Mac and immediately fell to the ground clutching your chest from a heart attack, you might not go back for that second bite. If your next puff of a cigarette instantly mutated your face into that of a weathered eighty-five-year-old, chances are you'd pass on that, too. If you failed to make that tenth call today and were immediately fired and bankrupted, suddenly picking up the phone would be a no-brainer. And, if that first forkful of cake instantly put fifty pounds on your frame, saying "no thank you" to dessert would be the true piece of cake.

The problem is that the payoff or instant gratification derived from bad habits often far outweighs what's going on in your rational mind concerning long-term consequences. Indulging in our bad habits doesn't seem to have any negative effects at all in the moment. You don't have that heart attack, your face doesn't shrivel up, you're not standing in the unemployment line, and your thighs aren't thunderous. But that doesn't mean you haven't activated the Compound Effect.

It's time to WAKE UP and realize that the habits you indulge in could be compounding your life into repeated disaster. The slightest adjustments to your daily routines can dramatically alter the outcomes in your life. Again, I'm not talking about quantum leaps of change or a complete overhaul of your personality, character, and life. Supersmall, seemingly inconsequential adjustments can and will revolutionize everything.

The best illustration I can give you to emphasize the power of small adjustments is that of a plane traveling from Los Angeles to New York City. If the nose of the plane is pointed only 1 percent off course—almost an invisible adjustment when the plane's sitting on the tarmac in Los Angeles—it will ultimately end up about 150 miles off course, arriving either upstate in Albany or in Dover, Delaware. Such is the case for your habits. A single poor habit, which doesn't look like much in the moment, can ultimately lead you miles off course from the direction of your goals and the life you desire. See Figure 6.

Most people drift through life without devoting much conscious energy to figuring out specifically what they want and what they need to do to take themselves there. I want to show you how to ignite your passion and help you aim your unstoppable creative power in the direction of your heart's dreams and desires. Uprooting bad habits that have grown into mighty oaks is going to be arduous and difficult; to see the process through will require something greater than even the most relentless determination—willpower alone won't cut it.

Fig. 6

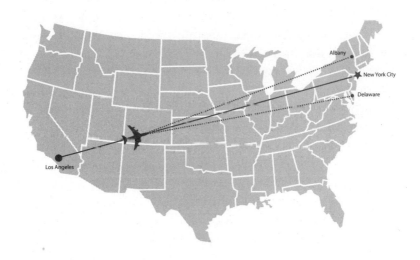

The power of small adjustments: a 1 percent change in course
results in being 150 miles off course.

Finding Your Mojo—Your Why-Power

Assuming willpower is what you need to change your
habits is akin to trying to keep a hungry grizzly bear out of
your picnic basket by covering it with a napkin. To fight the
bear of your bad habits, you need something stronger.

When you're having trouble doing the hard work of achieving
your goals, it's common to believe you simply lack willpower.
I disagree. It's not enough to choose to be successful. What's
going to keep you consistent with the new positive choices you

need to make? What's going to stop you from falling back into your mindless bad habits? What's going to be different this time versus the times you've tried and failed before? As soon as you get the slightest bit uncomfortable, you're going to be tempted to slide back into your old, comfortable routine.

You've tried willpower before and it's failed you. You've set resolutions and you've let them go. You thought you were going to lose all that weight last time. You thought you'd make all those sales calls last year. Let's "stop the insanity" and do something different so you can get different and *better* results.

Forget about willpower. It's time for *why-power*. Your choices are only meaningful when you connect them to your desires and dreams. The wisest and most motivating choices are the ones aligned with that which you identify as your purpose, your core self, and your highest values. You've got to want something, and know *why* you want it, or you'll end up giving up too easily.

So, what is your *why*? You've got to have a reason if you want to make significant improvements to your life. And to make you *want* to make the necessary changes, your *why* must be something that is fantastically motivating—to *you*. You've got to want to get up and go, go, go, go, go—for *years*! So, what is it that moves you the most? Identifying your why is critical. What *motivates you* is the ignition to your passion, the source for your enthusiasm, and the fuel of your persistence. This is so important that I made it the focus of another book, *Living Your Best Year Ever: A Proven System for Achieving BIG GOALS* (SUCCESS Books, 2011). You MUST know your *why*.

Why Everything's Possible

The power of your *why* is what gets you to stick through the grueling, mundane, and laborious. All of the *hows* will be meaningless until your *whys* are powerful enough. Until you've set your desire and motivation in place, you'll abandon any new path you seek to better your life. If your *why*-power— your desire—isn't great enough, if the fortitude of your commitment isn't powerful enough, you'll end up like every other person who makes a New Year's resolution and gives up too quickly and reverts to sleepwalking through poor choices. Let me give you an analogy to help bring it home:

If I were to put a ten-inch-wide, thirty-foot-long plank on the ground and say, "If you walk the length of the plank, I'll give you twenty dollars," would you do it? Of course, it's an easy twenty bucks. But what if I took that same plank and made a roof-top "bridge" between two 100-story buildings? That same twenty dollars for walking the thirty-foot plank no longer looks desirable or even possible, does it? You'd look at me and say, "Not on your life." See Figure 7.

However, if your child was on the opposite building, and that building was on fire, would you walk the length of the plank to save him? Without question and immediately—you'd do it, twenty dollars or not.

Fig. 7

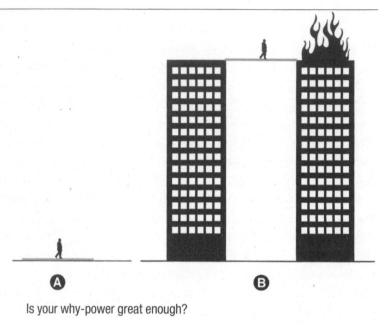

Is your why-power great enough?

Why is it that the first time I asked you to cross that sky-high plank, you said no way, yet, the second time you wouldn't hesitate? The risks and the dangers are the same. What changed? Your *why* changed—your reason for wanting to do it. You see, when the reason is big enough, you will be willing to perform almost any *how*.

To truly ignite your creative potential and inner drive, you have to look beyond the motivation of monetary and material goals. It's not that those motivations are bad; in fact, they're great. I'm a connoisseur of nice things. But material stuff can't really recruit your heart, soul, and guts into the fight. That passion has to come from a deeper place. And, even if you acquire the shiny object(s), you won't capture the real prize—happiness and fulfillment. In my interview with peak-performance expert Anthony Robbins (*SUCCESS*, January 2009), he said: "I have seen business moguls achieve their ultimate goals, but still live in frustration, worry, and fear. What's preventing these successful people from being happy? The answer is they have focused only on achievement and not fulfillment. Extraordinary accomplishment does not guarantee extraordinary joy, happiness, love, and a sense of meaning. These two skill sets feed off each other, and makes me believe that success without fulfillment is failure."

Well said. That's why it's not enough to choose to be successful. You have to dig deeper than that to find your core motivation, to activate your superpower. Your why-power.

Core Motivation

The access point to your why-power is through your *core values*, which define both who you are and what you stand for. Your core values are your internal compass, your guiding beacon, your personal GPS. They act as the filter through which you run all of life's demands, requests, and temptations, making sure they're leading you toward your intended destination. Getting your core values defined and properly calibrated is one of the most important steps in redirecting your life toward your grandest vision.

If you haven't already clearly defined your values, you may find yourself making choices that conflict with what you want. If, for example, honesty is a big thing for you, but you hang out with liars, there's a conflict. When your actions conflict with your values, you'll end up unhappy, frustrated, and despondent. In fact, psychologists tell us that nothing creates more stress than when our actions and behaviors aren't congruent with our values.

Defining your core values also helps make life simpler and more efficient. Decision-making is also easier when you are certain of your core values. When faced with a choice, ask yourself, "Does this align with my core values?" If it does, do it. If not, don't, and don't look back. All fretting and indecision are eliminated.

 To identify your core values, use the Core Values Assessment sheet on page 167, or download at www.TheCompoundEffect.com/free

---

Find Your Fight

People are either motivated by something they want or something they don't want. Love is a powerfully motivating force. But so is hate. Contrary to social correctness, it can be good to hate. Hate disease, hate injustice, hate ignorance, hate complacency, and so on. Sometimes identifying an enemy lights your fire. Some of my greatest motivation, determination, and dogged persistence came when I had an enemy to fight. In history, the most transformational stories and political revolutions came about as a result of fighting an enemy. David had Goliath. America had the British. Luke had Darth Vader. Rocky had Apollo Creed. Twenty-somethings have "The Man."

Rush Limbaugh has the Liberals. Lance Armstrong has cancer. Apple has Microsoft. Microsoft has Apple. We could go on and on, but you get the point.

Enemies give us a reason to stand tall with courage. Having to fight challenges your skills, your character, and your resolve. It forces you to assess and exercise your talents and abilities. Without a motivating fight, we can become fat and lazy; we lose our strength and purpose.

Some of my mentorship clients worry that their why-power derives from less-than-noble goals. They feel guilty for wanting to prove the naysayers wrong. Or wanting to get back at the person who said they'd never amount to anything, or beat the competition, or finally one-up a sibling who always dominated them. But, really, it doesn't matter what the motivation is (as long as it is legal and moral); you don't have to be motivated for great humanitarian reasons. What matters is that you feel fully motivated. Sometimes that motivation can help you use a powerfully negative emotion or experience to create an even more powerful and successful end.

This is certainly true of one of history's most celebrated football coaches, Pete Carroll. When we featured Carroll in *SUCCESS* magazine in September of 2008, he explained his early motivation like this: "When I grew up, I was a little dink. I couldn't do much because I was just too small. It took me a couple years to get in a place where I could be competitive. All that time, I was living with the fact that I was much better and I needed to fight to prove it. I was frustrated because I knew I could be special."

Carroll's need to fight ultimately brought out his greatness. Our March 2010 issue of *SUCCESS* magazine featured an interview with acclaimed actor Anthony Hopkins. I was surprised to learn that his extraordinary talent and determination blossomed from anger. Hopkins admitted to being a horrible student, burdened with dyslexia and attention-deficit hyperactivity disorder before such diagnoses existed. He was shackled with the label "problem child."

"I was a source of worry for my parents," Hopkins revealed. "I had no apparent future because schooling and education were important, but I didn't seem to have the ability to grasp what was being taught to me. My cousins were all brilliant; I felt resentful and rejected by a whole society and was very depressed."

Hopkins harnessed his anger. At first it propelled him to fight to achieve success outside of academics or athletics. He discovered he had a glimmer of talent in acting. So, he used his anger toward the belittling labels he'd been given to fuel his commitment to the craft of acting. Today, Hopkins is considered one of the greatest actors alive. As a result of the fame and fortune he's acquired, Hopkins has been able to help countless people in the fight to recover from substance abuse, in addition to supporting important environmental work. Though, initially, it wasn't grounded in a "noble" cause, his fight was clearly worthwhile.

We can all make powerful choices. We can all take back control by not blaming chance, fate, or anyone else for our outcomes. It's within our ability to cause everything to change. Rather than letting past hurtful experiences sap our energy and sabotage our success, we can use them to fuel positive, constructive change.

Goals

As I mentioned before, the Compound Effect is always working, and it will always take you somewhere. The question is, where? You can harness this relentless force and have it carry you to new heights. But you must know where you want to go. What goals, dreams, and destinations do you desire?

When I attended the funeral of Paul J. Meyer, another mentor of mine, I was reminded of the richness and diversity of his life. He achieved, experienced, and contributed more than dozens of people combined. His obituary made me reassess the quantity and size of the goals I set for myself. If Paul were here, he would tell us, "If you are not making the progress that you would like to make and are capable of making, it is simply because your goals are not clearly defined." One of Paul's most memorable quotes reminds us of the importance of goals: "Whatever you vividly imagine, ardently desire, sincerely believe, and enthusiastically act upon... must inevitably come to pass!"

The one skill most responsible for the abundance in my life is learning how to effectively set and achieve goals. Something almost magical happens when you organize and focus your creative power on a well-defined target. I've seen this time and again: the highest achievers in the world have all succeeded because they mapped out their visions. The person who has a clear, compelling, and white-hot burning why will always defeat even the best of the best at doing the *how*.

To figure out where you might need to add to or adjust your goals, take the Life Assessment on page 168, or download at www.TheCompoundEffect.com/free

How Goal Setting *Actually* Works: The Mystery 'Secret' Revealed

You only see, experience, and get what you look for. If you don't know what to look for, you certainly won't get it. By our very nature, we are goal-seeking creatures. Our brain is always trying to align our outer world with what we're seeing and expecting in our inner world. So, when you instruct your brain to look for the things you want, you will begin to see them. In fact, the object of your desire has probably always existed around you, but your mind and eyes weren't open to "seeing" it.

In reality, this is how the *Law of Attraction* really works. It is not the mysterious, esoteric voodoo it sometimes sounds like. It's far simpler and more practical than that.

We are bombarded with billions of sensory (visual, audio, physical) bites of information each day. To keep ourselves from going insane, we ignore 99.9 percent of them, only really seeing, hearing, or experiencing those upon which our mind focuses. This is why, when you "think" something, it appears that you are miraculously drawing it into your life. In reality, you're now just seeing what was already there. You are truly "attracting" it into your life. It wasn't there before or accessible to you until your thoughts focused and directed your mind to see it.

Make sense? This isn't mysterious at all; it's, in fact, quite logical. Now, with this new perception, whatever your mind is thinking internally is what it will focus on and all of a sudden "see" within that 99.9 percent of remaining space.

Here's a well-worn example (because it's so true!): In shopping for or buying a new car, you suddenly start to see that model and make everywhere, right? It seems like there are tons of them on the streets all of a sudden when they weren't there yesterday. But is that realistic? Of course not. They were there all along, but you weren't paying attention to them. Thus, they didn't really "exist" to you until you gave them your attention.

When you define your goals, you give your brain something new to look for and focus on. It's as if you're giving your mind a new set of eyes from which to see all the people, circumstances, conversations, resources, ideas, and creativity surrounding you. With this new perspective (an inner itinerary), your mind proceeds to match up on the outside what you want most on the inside—your goal. It's that simple. The difference in how you experience the world and draw ideas, people, and opportunities into your life after you have clearly defined your goals is profound.

In one of my interviews with Brian Tracy, he put it this way: "Top people have very clear goals. They know who they are and they know what they want. They write it down and they make plans for its accomplishment. Unsuccessful people carry their goals around in their head like marbles rattling around in a can, and we say a goal that is not in writing is merely a fantasy. And everybody has fantasies, but those fantasies are like bullets with no powder in the cartridge. People go through life shooting blanks without written goals—and that's the starting point."

I suggest that you take some time *today* to make a list of your most important goals. I recommend considering goals in all aspects of your life, not just for your business or finances. Be wary of the high price of putting too much focus on any single aspect of your life, to the exclusion of everything else. Go for whole-life success—balance in all the aspects of life that are important to you: business, finances, health and well-being, spirituality, family and relationships, and lifestyle.

 The system I have used has now been made available to the public in the program *Living Your Best Year Ever– A Proven System for Achieving BIG Goals* available at www.SUCCESS.com/BestYearEver.

Who You Have to Become

When most people set out to achieve new goals, they ask, "Okay, I have my goal; now what do I need to *do* to get it?" It's not a bad question, but it's not the first question that needs to be addressed either. The question we should be asking ourselves is: "Who do I need to become?" You probably know some people who seem to do all the right things, but still don't produce the results they want, right? Why not? One thing Jim Rohn taught me is: "If you want to have more, you have to *become* more. Success is not something you pursue. What you pursue will elude you; it can be like trying to chase butterflies. Success is something you attract by the person you become."

When I understood that philosophy, wow! It revolutionized

my life and personal growth. When I was single and ready to find my mate and get married, I made a long list of traits I desired in the perfect woman (for me). I filled more than forty pages of a journal, front and back, describing her in great detail—her personality, character, key attributes, attitudes, and philosophies about life, even what kind of family she'd come from, including her culture and physical makeup, down to the texture of her hair. I wrote in depth what our life would be like and what we'd do together. If I had then asked, "What do I have to *do* to find and get this girl?" I might still be on that butterfly chase. Instead, I looked back at the list and considered whether or not I embodied those same attributes myself. Did I have the very qualities I was expecting in her? I asked myself, "What kind of a man would a woman like this be looking for? Who do I need to become to be attractive to a woman of this substance?"

I filled forty more pages describing all the attributes, qualities, behaviors, attitudes, and characteristics I needed to become myself. Then I went to work on becoming and achieving those qualities. Guess what? It worked! As if she were peeled off the pages of my journal and appeared in front of me, my wife, Georgia, is exactly what I described and asked for, in almost eerie detail. The key was my getting clear on who I'd have to be to attract and keep a woman of her quality, and then doing the work to achieve that.

 To identify bad habits and needed new habits essential to becoming and achieving what you want, complete the Habit Assessment sheet on page 169, or download at www.TheCompoundEffect.com/free

---

Behave Yourself

Alright, let's map out your process for achieving the goals you've decided upon. This is the *doing* process—or, in some cases, the *STOP-doing* process.

What stands between you and your goal is your *behavior*. Do you need to stop doing anything so the Compound Effect isn't taking you into a downward spiral? Similarly, what do you need to start doing to change your trajectory so that it's headed in the most beneficial direction? In other words, what habits and behaviors do you need to subtract from and add to your life?

Your life comes down to this formula:

YOU → CHOICE + BEHAVIOR + HABIT + COMPOUNDED = GOALS
　　　　(decision)　　(action)　(repeated action)　　(time)

That's why it's imperative to figure out which behaviors are blocking the path that leads to your goal, and which behaviors will help you accomplish your goal.

You may think you've got a handle on all your bad habits, but I'd bet good money you're wrong. Again, that's why tracking is so effective. I mean, honestly, do you know how many hours of TV you really watch every day? How many hours do you spend tuned to news channels or keeping up with the goals and accomplishments of others on the sports or style networks? Do you know how many cans of soda you drink? Or how many hours you spend doing nonessential "work" on the computer (Facebook, reading online gossip, etc.)? As I emphasized in the previous chapter, your first job is to become aware of how you're behaving. Where have you fallen asleep on the job and developed an unconscious bad habit that's leading you astray?

Not long ago, a successful executive with whom I serve on a nonprofit board hired me to mentor him on improving his productivity. He was doing well, but knew he could optimize his time and output further with some coaching. I had him track his activities for a week, and I noticed something I see too often: He spent an incredible amount of time reviewing the news—forty-five minutes in the morning reading the newspaper, another thirty minutes listening to news on his morning commute, and an equal amount of time tuning in again on his drive back home. During his workday, he'd check Yahoo! News several times, spending at least twenty minutes in total. When he got home, he'd catch the last fifteen minutes of the local news while greeting his family. Then he'd catch up on thirty minutes of sports news and thirty minutes of the 10 o'clock news before going to bed. In total, he was spending 3.5 hours with the news each day! This man wasn't an economist or a commodities trader, or in any profession that lived or died by the latest news. The time he spent with the paper and news programs on radio and TV greatly exceeded what he needed to be a knowledgeable voter and contributing member of society, or even to enhance his own personal interests. In fact, he was getting very little valuable information through his programming choices—or, rather, his *lack* of choices. So why did he spend nearly four hours a day consuming it? It was a habit.

I suggested he keep his TV and radio off, cancel his newspaper subscription, and set up an RSS feeder so he could select and receive only the news he deemed important for his business and personal interests. Doing so immediately cleared out 95 percent of the mind-cluttering and time-sucking noise. He could now review all that mattered to him in less than twenty minutes a day. This left the forty-five minutes in the morning (his commute time), and that hour in the evening for productive activities: exercise, listening to instructional and inspirational material, reading, planning, preparing, and spending quality time with his family. He tells me he's never felt less stressed (constant negative news has a tendency to make you anxious), and more inspired and focused than he does now. One small, simple change in habit, one giant leap forward in balance and productivity!

Okay, now it's your turn. Get out your little notebook and write out your top three goals. Now make a list of the bad habits that might be sabotaging your progress in each area. *Write down every one.*

Habits and behaviors never lie. If there's a discrepancy between what you say and what you do, I'm going to believe what you *do* every time. If you tell me you want to be healthy, but you've got Doritos dust on your fingers, I'm believing the Doritos. If you say self-improvement is a priority, but you spend more time with your Xbox than at the library, I'm believing the Xbox. If you say you're a dedicated professional, but you show up late and unprepared, your behavior rats you out every time. You say your family is your top priority, but if they don't appear on your busy calendar, they aren't, really. Look at the list of bad habits you just made. That's the truth about who you are. Now you get to decide whether that's okay, or if you want to change.

Next, add to that list all the habits you need to adopt that, practiced and compounded over time, will result in you gloriously achieving your goals.

Making this list isn't about wasting energy by getting judgmental and regretful. It's about taking a clear-headed look at what you want to improve. I'm not going to leave you there, however. Let's uproot those sabotaging bad habits and plant new, positive, and healthy ones in their place.

Game Changers: Five Strategies for Eliminating Bad Habits

Your habits are learned; therefore, they can be unlearned. If you want to sail your life in a new direction, you have to first pick up the anchors of bad habits that have been weighing you down. The key is to make your why-power so strong that it overwhelms your urges for instant gratification. And for that, you need a new game plan. The following are my all-time favorite game changers:

1. Identify Your Triggers

Look at your list of bad habits. For each one you've written down, identify what triggers it. Figure out what I call "The Big 4's"—the "who," the "what," the "where," and the "when" underlying each bad behavior. For example:

- Are you more likely to drink too much when you're with certain people?
- Is there a particular time of day when you just *have* to have something sweet?
- What emotions tend to provoke your worst habits—stress, fatigue, anger, nervousness, boredom?
- When do you experience those emotions? Who are you with, where are you, or what are you doing?

- What situations prompt your bad habits to surface—getting in your car, the time before performance reviews, visits with your in-laws? Conferences? Social settings? Feeling physically insecure? Deadlines?
- Take a closer look at your routines. What do you typically say when you wake up? When you're on a coffee or lunch break? When you've gotten home from a long day?

Again, get out your notebook or use the Bad Habit Killer Worksheet here (which you can also download for free at www.TheCompoundEffect.com/free) and write down your triggers. This simple action alone increases your awareness exponentially. But, of course, this isn't the whole enchilada, because as we've discussed, increasing your awareness of a bad habit isn't enough to break it.

2. Clean House

Get to scrubbin'. And I mean this literally and figuratively. If you want to stop drinking alcohol, remove every drop of it from your house (and your vacation house, if you have one). Get rid of the glasses, any fancy utensils or doo-dads you use when you drink, and those decorative olives, too. If you want to stop drinking coffee, heave the coffee maker, and give that bag of gourmet grounds to a sleepy neighbor. If you're trying to curb your spending, take an evening and cancel every catalogue or retail offer that flies in through your mailbox or your inbox, so you won't even need to muster the discipline to walk it from the front door to the recycle bin. If you want to eat more healthfully, clean your cupboards of all the crap, stop buying the junk food—and stop buying into the argument that it's "not fair" to deny the other people in your family junk food just because you don't want it in your life. Trust me; everyone in your family is better off without it. Don't bring it into the house, period. Get rid of whatever enables your bad habits.

3. Swap It

Look again at your list of bad habits. How can you alter them so that they're not as harmful? Can you replace them with healthier habits or drop-kick them altogether? As in, for good.

Anyone who knows me knows that I love something sweet after a meal. If there is ice cream in the house, the something sweet turns into a triple-scoop banana split with all the fixings (1,255 calories). Instead, I replace that bad habit with two Hershey's Kisses (50 calories). I'm still able to satisfy the sweet tooth without having to spend the extra hour on the treadmill just to get back to even.

My sister-in-law started a habit of eating crunchy and salty junk food when she watched TV. She'd crunch through a whole bag of tortilla chips with little actual awareness. Then she realized that what she really enjoyed was the crunchy sensation in her mouth. She decided to replace her bad habit with crunching on carrot and celery sticks, and raw broccoli spears. She got the same joyful sensation, and her FDA-recommended vegetable servings at the same time.

A guy who used to work for me had a habit of drinking eight to ten Diet Cokes a day (that's a BAD habit!). I suggested he replace them with low-sodium, carbonated water, adding fresh lemon, lime, or oranges. He did this for about a month before realizing he didn't need the carbonation at all, and switched to just plain water.

Play with this, and see what behaviors you can replace, delete, or swap out.

4. Ease In

I live near the Pacific Ocean. Whenever I get in the water, I get my ankles acclimated first, then walk in up to my knees, then it's my waist and chest, before taking the plunge. Some people just run and dive in and get it over with—good for them. Not me. I like to ease my way in (probably residual trauma from my childhood, as you'll see in the next strategy). For some of your long-standing and deep-rooted habits, it may be more effective to take small steps to ease into unwinding them. You may have spent decades repeating, cementing, and fortifying those habits, so it can be wise to give yourself some time to unravel them, one step at a time.

A few years, ago my wife's doctor required she cut out caffeine from her diet for several months. We both *love* our coffee, so if she was going to have to suffer, I decided it was only fair that we do it together. We first went to 50/50—50 percent decaffeinated and 50 percent regular for a week. Then 100 percent decaf for another week. Then Earl Grey decaf tea for a week, followed by decaf green tea. It took us a month to get there, but we didn't suffer even a moment of caffeine withdrawal—no headaches, no sleepiness, no brain fog, no nothing. However, if we had gone cold turkey… well, I shiver at the thought.

5. Or Jump In

Not everyone is wired the same way. Some researchers have found that it can be paradoxically easier for people to make lifestyle changes if they change a great many bad habits at once. For example, pioneering cardiologist Dr. Dean Ornish found he could reverse people's advanced heart disease—without medication or surgery—with dramatic lifestyle changes. He discovered they often found it easier to say goodbye to almost all their bad habits at once. He enrolled them in a training session where he substituted a very low-fat diet for their fat- and cholesterol-rich fare. The program included exercise— getting them off their couches and walking or jogging—as well as stress-reduction techniques, and other heart-healthy habits. Amazingly, in less than a month, these patients learned to let go of a lifetime of bad habits and embrace new ones—and they went on to experience dramatic health benefits after a year as a result. Personally, I find this to be the exception, not the rule, but you'll have to figure out the strategy that works best for you.

When I was a kid, my family camped at a little-known spot called Lake Rollins. The lake, situated not far from the Sierras in Northern California, is fed from glaciers that melt from atop the mountains of Lake Tahoe. The water's ridiculously cold. Every day we were there, my dad insisted that I water ski in the polar pond. All day I would be quietly anxious about the dreaded call to go in. I loved to water ski; I just hated getting *in* the water. A slight conflict of interest, because of course, there was no separating one from the other.

Dad made sure that I never missed my turn, sometimes by actually physically throwing me in. After a dozen or so excruciating seconds of near-hypothermia, I always found the water refreshing and rejuvenating. My anticipation of getting in the water was actually worse than the reality of just jumping in. Once my body acclimated, water skiing was a blast. And, yet, I went through this cycle of dread and relief each and every time.

That experience isn't unlike that of suddenly dropping or changing a bad habit. For a short while it can feel excruciating, or at least quite uncomfortable. But just as the body adjusts to a changing environment through a process called homeostasis, we have a similar homeostatic ability to adjust to unfamiliar behavior changes. And usually, we can regulate ourselves physiologically and psychologically to the new circumstances quite quickly.

Sometimes wading in just won't do. Sometimes you really do have to jump in. I want you to ask yourself now, "Where can I start slow and hold myself accountable?" And, "Where do I need to take that bigger leap? Where have I been avoiding pain or discomfort, when I know deep down that I'll adapt in no time if I just go for it?"

One of my former partners has a brother who was a beer-guzzling, bar-brawling, life-of-the-party alcoholic. He drank at lunch, with dinner, after dinner, and all weekend long. One day he was at a wedding for a former college roommate when he saw his friend's brother, who was ten years older than both of them, but looked ten years younger! He watched the man dance, laugh, and play during the wedding, exuding a vitality he hadn't felt in many years. He made a decision on the spot that he would never touch a drop of alcohol again. Cold turkey, that was it, never again. And he hasn't in more than six years.

When it comes to changing bad habits at home, I'm a toe dipper. But in my professional life, I find that taking the big plunge is far more effective. Whether committing to a new business or dealing with potential new clients, partners, or investors, toe dipping usually doesn't cut it. Each time, I think of Lake Rollins and know it will be painful at first, but I remember that within little time, it will be exhilarating, and well worth the temporary discomfort.

Run a Vice Check

I'm not suggesting you cut out every "bad" thing in your life. Most everything is good in moderation. But, how can you tell whether a bad habit is becoming the boss of you? I believe in testing my vices. Every so often I go on a "vice fast." I pick one vice, and check to be sure I'm still the alpha dog in our relationship. My vices are coffee, ice cream, wine, and movies. I already told you about my ice cream obsession. When it comes to wine, I want to be sure I'm enjoying a glass and celebrating the day, not drowning a bad mood.

About every three months, I pick one vice and abstain for thirty days (this probably stems from my Catholic Lent upbringing). I love proving to myself that I'm still in charge. Try this yourself. Pick a vice—something you do in moderation, but you know doesn't contribute to your highest good—and take yourself on a thirty-day wagon run. If you find it seriously difficult to abstain for those thirty days, you may have found a habit worth cutting out of your life.

Game Changers:
Six Techniques for Installing Good Habits

Now that we have helped you eliminate the bad habits that are taking you in the wrong direction, we need to create new choices, behaviors, and ultimately habits that will finally take you in the direction of your grandest desires. Eliminating a bad habit means removing something from your routine. Installing a new, more productive habit requires an entirely different skill set. You're planting the tree, watering it, fertilizing it, and making sure it's properly rooted. Doing so takes effort, time, and practice. Here are my favorite techniques for putting good habits in place.

Leadership expert John C. Maxwell said, "You will never change your life until you change something you do daily. The secret of your success is found in your daily routine." According to research, it takes three hundred instances of positive reinforcement to turn a new habit into an unconscious practice—that's almost a year of daily practice! Fortunately, as we talked about earlier, we know we've got a much better chance of cementing a new habit into our lives after three weeks of diligent focus. That means that if we bring special attention to a new habit *daily* for the first three weeks, we have a far better chance of making it a lifelong practice.

The truth is, you can change a habit in a second, or you can still be trying to break it after ten long years. The first time you touched a hot stove, you instantly knew you'd never make that a habit! The shock and pain was so intense that it forever changed your awareness; you knew you'd be conscious for the rest of your life around hot stoves.

The key is staying aware. If you really want to maintain a good habit, make sure you pay attention to it at least once a day, and you're far more likely to succeed.

1. Set Yourself Up to Succeed

Any new habit has to work inside your life and lifestyle. If you join a gym that's thirty miles away, you won't go. If you're a night owl but the gym closes at 6 p.m., it won't work for you. Your gym must be close and convenient, and fit into your schedule. If you want to lose weight and eat healthier, make sure your fridge and pantry are stocked with healthy options. Want to make sure you don't binge on vending machine snacks when you get midday hunger pangs? Keep nuts and healthy snacks in your desk drawer. The easiest thing to grab when you're hungry is empty carbs. One strategy I use is to have protein on hand. I cook up a bunch of chicken on Sunday, and package it and have it ready for the week.

One of my most distracting and destructive habits is my e-mail addiction. Seriously, this is no laughing matter. I can lose hours of focus every day with the massive amounts of e-mail flooding my inbox if I'm not vigilant about staying organized and focused. To set up the discipline of my new habit of only checking e-mail three times a day, I turned off all alarms, all automatic-receive functions, and shut the program down when I'm not in one of those three windows of allocated time. I have to build the walls around that time vortex, lest I keep falling in all day.

2. Think Addition, Not Subtraction

When I interviewed Montel Williams for *SUCCESS*, he told me about the strict diet he maintains because of the disease that afflicts him, multiple sclerosis. Montel has adopted something called "The Add-in Principle," and I think it's a wildly effective tool for anyone with any goal.

"It's not so much what you attempt to take out of your diet," he explained to me. "It's what you *put in* instead." This has become his analogy for life. Instead of thinking that he has to deprive himself, or take something out of his diet (e.g., "I can't eat a hamburger, chocolate, or dairy"), he thinks about what he *can* have instead (e.g., "Today I'm going to have a salad and steamed vegetables and fresh figs"). He fills his focus and his belly with what he can have, so he no longer has attention or hunger for what he can't. Instead of focusing on what he has to sacrifice, Montel thinks about what he gets to "add in." The result is a lot more powerful.

A friend of mine wanted to break his bad habit of wasting too much time watching TV. To help out, I asked him what he'd like to do with three hours of free time if he had it. He said he would play with his kids more. I also asked him to pick a hobby he'd always wanted to explore. His choice was photography. A total techie, he went out and got all this high-tech editing equipment, which he happily toted along on more family outings so he could take great photos of his kids. Then he'd spend hours in the evening editing and putting together slide shows and photo albums for the whole family to enjoy. They ended up spending time together, laughing and remembering how much fun they'd had. Because he was so focused on his kids and photography, he no longer had the time nor the desire to sit around and watch TV at night. He realized he'd been zoning out on it because it was an easy mental escape from his workday. By replacing TV viewing with his new habit of playing games with his kids and working on his photography hobby he discovered passions with far more power and far bigger payoffs.

What can you choose to "add in" so you can enrich your life experience?

3. Go for a PDA: Public Display of Accountability

Picture any public official taking the oath of office. "I do solemnly swear..." and then comes the speech on how she'll turn her campaign promises into boots-on-the-ground realities. Once she puts it out there on the public record, she knows that she'll be held responsible for any action that rolls back on her promises and praised for any progress toward her goals.

Want to cement that new habit? Get Big Brother to watch you. It's never been easier with all the social media available. I heard about one woman who decided to get control of her finances by blogging about every penny she spends every day. She's got her family, friends, and plenty of colleagues following her spending habits, and as a result of the many eyes of scrutiny, she's become far more responsible and disciplined in her finances.

I once helped a co-worker quit smoking by telling everyone at the company: "Listen up! Zelda's decided to stop smoking! Isn't that great? She just smoked her last cigarette!" I then placed a huge wall calendar on the outside of her cubical. Every day she didn't smoke, Zelda got to draw a big fat red X on the calendar. Co-workers took notice and started to cheer her on, and the parade of big red X's started to fill up the chart, which took on a life of its own. Zelda didn't want to quit on that chart, quit on her co-workers, or quit on herself. But she did quit smoking!

Tell your family. Tell your friends. Tell Facebook and Twitter. Get the word out that there's a new sheriff in town, and you're in charge.

4. Find a Success Buddy

There are few things as powerful as two people locked arm and arm marching toward the same goal. To up your chances of success, get a success buddy, someone who'll keep you accountable as you cement your new habit while you return the favor. I, for example, have what I call a "Peak-Performance Partner." Every Friday at 11 a.m. sharp, we have a thirty-minute call during which we trade our wins, losses, fixes, ah-has, and solicit the needed feedback and hold each other accountable. You might seek out a success buddy for regular walks, runs, or dates at the gym, or to meet to discuss and trade personal-development books.

5. Competition & Camaraderie

There's nothing like a friendly contest to whet your competitive spirit and immerse yourself in a new habit with a bang. Dr. Mehmet Oz once told me in an interview, "If people would just walk a thousand more steps per day, they would change their lives". VideoPlus, the parent company for *SUCCESS*, held a step competition using shoe pedometers to count steps. Employees organized into teams and competed to see which team could accumulate the most steps. It was amazing to me that people who didn't previously exercise for their own health or benefit suddenly started walking four, five, or six miles a day! At lunch, they walked in the parking lot. If they knew they had a conference call, suddenly they were out doing it on their cell phones while they walked! Because of the competition, they found ways to increase their activity. Everyone's steps were tracked, and the whole office could see who was slacking off and who was stepping up. People's step tallies increased every day.

Yet as soon as the competition was over, I was fascinated to observe that the step count completely dropped off the cliff— by more than 60 percent just one month after the competition. When the competition was reorganized again, the step count shot right back up. All it took was a little competition to keep people's engines revved—and they got a wonderful sense of community and shared experience and camaraderie in the bargain.

What kind of friendly competition can you organize with your friends, colleagues, or teammates? How can you inject fun rivalry and a competitive spirit into your new habit?

6. Celebrate!

All work and no play make Jack a dull boy, and it's a recipe for backsliding. There should be a time to celebrate, to enjoy some of the fruits of your victories along the way. You can't go through this thing sacrificing yourself with no benefit. You've got to find little rewards to give yourself every month, every week, every day—even something small to acknowledge that you've held yourself to a new behavior. Maybe time to yourself to take a walk, relax in the bath, or read something just for fun. For bigger milestones, book a massage or have dinner at your favorite restaurant. And promise yourself a nice big pot of gold when you reach the end of the rainbow.

Change Is Hard: Yippee!

There is a one thing that 99 percent of "failures" and "successful" folks have in common—they all hate doing the same things. The difference is successful people do them anyway. Change is hard. That's why people don't transform their bad habits, and why so many people end up unhappy and unhealthy.

What excites me about this reality, however, is that if change were easy, and everyone were doing it, it would be much more difficult for you and me to stand out and become an extraordinary success. Ordinary is easy. *Extra*-ordinary is what will separate you from the crowd.

Personally, I'm always happy when something is hard. Why? Because I know that most people won't do what it takes; therefore, it will be easier for me to step in front of the pack and take the lead. I love what Dr. Martin Luther King Jr. said so eloquently: "The ultimate measure of a man is not where he stands in moments of comfort and convenience, but where he stands at times of challenge." When you press on despite difficulty, tedium, and hardship, that's when you earn your improvement and gain strides on the competition. If it's hard, awkward, or tedious, so be it. Just do it. And keep doing it, and the magic of the Compound Effect will reward you handsomely.

Be Patient

When it comes to breaking old bad habits and starting new ones, remember to be patient with yourself. If you've spent twenty, thirty, or forty years or more repeating the behaviors you're now trying to change, you've got to expect it's going to take time and effort before you see lasting results. Science shows that patterns of thoughts and actions repeated many times create what's called a neuro-signature or a "brain groove," or a series of interconnected neurons that carry the thought patterns of a particular habit. Attention feeds the habit. When we give our attention to a habit, we activate the brain groove, releasing the thoughts, desires, and actions related to that habit. Luckily, our brains are malleable. If we stop giving attention to the bad habits, those grooves weaken. When we form new habits, we drive new grooves deeper with each repetition, eventually overpowering the previous ones.

Creating new habits (and burning new grooves into your brain) will take time. Be patient with yourself. If you fall off the wagon, brush yourself off (not beat yourself up!), and get back on. No problem. We all stumble. Just go again and try another strategy; reinforce your commitment and consistency. When you press on, you will receive huge payoffs. Speaking of payoffs, the next chapter is where we really start breaking away from the herd, where the multiplying effect really takes shape. With all the disciplined effort you've applied from the fundamentals of the first three chapters, here's where you get rewarded—big time!

Put the Compound Effect to Work for You

Summary Action Steps

↗ Identify your three best habits—those that support your most important goal.

Identify your three bad habits that take you off course from your most important goal.

↗ Identify three new habits you need to develop to put you on track toward your most important goal. Download the Habits sheet at www.TheCompoundEffect.com/free

↗ Identify your core motivation. Discover what gets you fired up and keeps you fired up to achieve big results. Download the Core Values Assessment document at www.TheCompoundEffect.com/free

↗ Find your why-power. Design your concise, compelling, and awe-inspiring goals. Download the goal sheet at www.TheCompoundEffect.com/free

↗ Order your copy of *Living Your Best Year Ever–A Proven System for Achieving BIG GOALS* from www.SUCCESS.com/BestYearEver to guide you through the designing process as well as the achieving process all year long.

CHAPTER 4

MOMENTUM

I'd like to introduce you to a very good friend of mine. This friend, also close to Bill Gates, Steve Jobs, Richard Branson, Michael Jordan, Lance Armstrong, Michael Phelps, and every other superachiever, will impact your life like no other. I'd like to introduce you to Mo, or "Big Mo," as I like to call it. Big Mo is, without doubt, one of the most powerful and enigmatic forces of success. You can't see or feel Mo, but you know when you've got it. You can't count on Mo showing up to every occasion, but when it does—WOW! Big Mo can catapult you into the stratosphere of success. And once you've got Mo on your side, there's almost no way anyone can catch you.

I'm excited about this chapter. When you implement the ideas outlined ahead, your payoff will be a thousand times (or more) what you paid for this book. Seriously, these ideas are BIG!

Harnessing the Power of Big Mo

If you remember your high-school physics class (you do, don't you?), you'll recall Newton's First Law, also known as the *Law of Inertia*: Objects at rest tend to stay at rest unless acted on by an outside force. Objects in motion tend to stay in motion, unless something stops their momentum. Put another way, couch potatoes tend to stay couch potatoes. Achievers—people who get into a successful rhythm—continue busting their butts and end up achieving more and more.

It's not easy to build momentum, but once you do, look out! Do you remember playing on merry-go-rounds when you were a kid? A bunch of your friends piled on, weighing the thing down and then chanted as you worked to get the thing moving. Getting started was slow going. The first step was always the hardest—getting it to move from a standstill. You had to push and pull, grimace and groan and throw your entire your body into the effort. One step, two steps, three steps—it seemed like you were getting nowhere. After a long and hard effort, finally you were able to get up a little bit of speed and run along side it. Even though you were moving (and your friends were cheering louder), to get the speed you really wanted, you had to keep running faster and faster, pulling it behind you as you ran with all your might. Finally, success! You jumped on and joined your friends in the joy of feeling the wind in your face and watching the outside world turn into a smear of colors. After a while, when the merry-go-round started to slow down, you'd hop off and run alongside for a minute to get the speed back up—or you could simply give it a couple good pushes and then hop back on. Once the merry-go-round was spinning at a good clip, momentum took over, making it easy to keep it going.

Adopting any change is the same way. You get started by taking one small step, one action at a time. Progress is slow, but once a newly formed habit has kicked in, Big Mo joins the party. Your success and results compound rapidly. See Figure 8.

Fig. 8

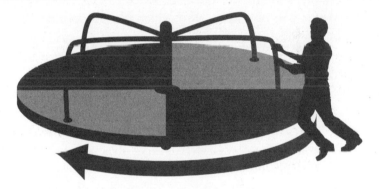

It takes time and energy to get Big Mo, but with it, success and results compound rapidly.

The same thing happens when a rocket ship launches. The space shuttle uses more fuel during the first few minutes of its flight than it does the rest of the entire trip. Why? Because it has to break free from the pull of gravity. Once it does, it can glide in orbit. The hard part? Getting off the ground. Your old ways and your old conditioning are just like the inertia of the merry-go-round or the pull of gravity. Everything just wants to stay at rest. You'll need a lot of energy to break your inertia and get your new enterprise under way. But once you get momentum, you will be hard to stop—virtually unbeatable—even though you're now putting out considerably less effort while receiving greater results.

Ever wonder why successful people tend to get more successful... the rich get richer... the happy get happier... the lucky get luckier?

They've got Mo. When it rains, it pours.

But momentum works on both sides of the equation—it can work for you or against you. Since the Compound Effect is *always* working, negative habits, when left unchecked, can build up steam and send you into a tailspin of "unlucky" circumstances and consequences. That's what our friend Brad from Chapter 1 experienced. He gained thirty-three pounds with a few small bad habits, and experienced major job and marriage stress because of the negative momentum those habits generated. The law of inertia says objects at rest tend to stay at rest—that's the Compound Effect working *against* you. The more time you spend sitting on that couch watching *Two and a Half Men*, the harder it will be for you to get up and get moving. So let's start RIGHT NOW!

How do you get Big Mo to pay you a visit? You build up to it. You get into the groove, the "zone," by doing the things we've covered so far:

1) Making new choices based on your goals and core values
2) Putting those choices to work through new positive behaviors
3) Repeating those healthy actions long enough to establish new habits
4) Building routines and rhythms into your daily disciplines
5) Staying consistent over a long enough period of time

Then, BANG! Big Mo kicks in your door (that's a good thing)! And you're virtually unstoppable.

Think about swimmer Michael Phelps, who won a legendary eight gold medals at the 2008 Summer Olympics in Beijing. How did he do it? Working with his coach, Bob Bowman, Phelps honed his talents over the course of twelve years. Together, they built routines and rhythms, and developed a consistency of performance that prepared Phelps to catch momentum just at the right time—the Olympic Games. Phelps and Bowman's symbiotic relationship is legendary for its scope and ambition—and its utter predictability. Bowman required such consistency when it came to practice that one of Phelps' most vivid memories is when Bowman allowed him to finish a training session *15 minutes early* so he could get ready for a middle-school dance! That's one time in twelve years! No wonder Phelps was so unbeatable in the pool!

Chances are you have an iPod. Ever think about the evolution that made it possible for that little gizmo to wind up in your pocket? Apple was around a long time before they launched the iPod. While Mac computers have always had an intensely loyal following, they still comprise a small fraction of the overall PC market. The iPod certainly wasn't the first MP3 player out there; Apple was actually late to the game. But they had something powerful going for them: the consistency of their efforts in maintaining customer loyalty, a steadfast commitment to high quality, innovative design, and ease of use. They made the MP3 player simple, cool, easy to use and play with, and promoted it through entertaining and inventive ad campaigns. It worked! It hit a nerve.

But, the iPod wasn't an overnight success. In 2001, the year

Apple released the iPod, they went from 30 percent revenue growth the year previous to -33 percent. The following year, 2002, was also a negative revenue growth year at -2 percent. But 2003 saw a shift to a positive 18 percent. Growth came again in 2004, up to 33 percent. And in 2005, they caught Mo, and BANG! Apple catapulted to 68 percent revenue growth and now holds more than 70 percent of the MP3 player market share. As you know, Big Mo has since helped them dominate the smartphone market (with the iPhone) and digital music distribution with iTunes. This momentum has also given them a resurgence of growth in their original market of personal computers. With Big Mo on their side, I wouldn't be surprised to see them expand into other markets.

Google was a small, struggling search engine for a while; today it, too, owns more than 60 percent of its market. YouTube, the video-sharing space created in February 2005, officially launched in November of that year. But it wasn't until they featured the "Lazy Sunday" digital short that originally aired on *Saturday Night Live* that people started going to YouTube in huge numbers to find it. That YouTube video clip went viral—it got more than 5 million views before NBC asked to have it taken down. Then, there was no way to catch them—they had Mo. Today YouTube owns more than 60 percent of the video market! Google caught up with You Tube's two young founders and paid them $1.65 billion to buy their Mo. Wow!

What do Michael Phelps, Apple, Google, and YouTube have in common? They were doing the same things before and after they achieved momentum. Their habits, disciplines, routines, and consistency were the keys that unlocked momentum for each. And they became *unstoppable* when Big Mo showed up to their party.

Routine Power

Some of our best intentions fail because we don't have a system of execution. When it comes down to it, your new attitudes and behaviors must be incorporated into your monthly, weekly, and daily routines to affect any real, positive change. A routine is something you do every day without fail, so that eventually, like brushing your teeth or putting on your seatbelt, you do it without conscious thought. Similar to our discussion in the Habits section, if you look at anything you do that's successful, you'll see that you've probably developed a routine for it. These routines ease life's stresses by making our actions automatic and effective. To reach new goals and develop new habits, it's necessary to create new routines to support your objectives.

The greater the challenge, the more rigorous our routines need to be. Ever wonder why military boot camp is so hard—where relatively minor tasks like making the bed, shining your shoes, or standing at attention become over-the-top important? Building routines to prep soldiers for combat is the most effective way to elicit efficient, productive, and reliable performance under intense pressure. The seemingly simplistic routines built and developed during basic training are so exact that soft, fearful, slovenly teenagers are transformed into lean, confident, mission-driven soldiers in only eight to twelve weeks. Their routines are so well-rehearsed that these young soldiers can instinctively act with precision in the middle of the chaos of combat. That intense level of training and practice prepares soldiers to carry out their duties—even under the threat of imminent death.

Now, your days might not be as dangerous, but without

the proper routines built into your schedule, the results of your life can be unruly and unnecessarily hard. Developing a routine of predictable, daily disciplines prepares you to be victorious on the battlefield of life.

Golfer Jack Nicklaus was famous for his pre-shot routine. He was religious about the "dance" he would do before every shot, a series of routine mental and physical steps that got him fully focused and ready for the shot. Jack would start out behind the ball, and then pick out one or two intermediate spots between the ball and the target. As he walked around and approached the ball, the first thing he would do is line up his clubface to his intermediate target. He wouldn't put his feet into position until he felt he had his clubface properly squared up. Then he would take his stance. From there, he would waggle the club and look out to his target, then back to his intermediate target and back to the golf club, with a repeat of the view. Then, and only then, would he strike the ball.

During one of the important Majors, a psychologist timed Nicklaus from the moment he pulled the club out of the bag until the moment he hit the ball, and guess what? In each shot, from the first tee to the eighteenth green, the timing of Jack's routine supposedly *never* varied more than *one* second. That is amazing! The same psychologist measured Greg Norman during his unfortunate collapse at the 1996 Masters. Lo and behold, his pre-shot routine got faster and faster as the round progressed. Varying his routine stunted his rhythm and consistency; he was never able to catch momentum. The moment Norman changed his routine, his performance became unpredictable and his results erratic.

Football kickers likewise cherish their pre-kick routines, which allow them to get into sync with the thousands of times they have done this same action. Predictably, without a pre-kick routine, their performance under time pressure greatly diminishes. Pilots go through their preflight checklist. Even when a pilot has logged thousands of hours and the plane just came in with a "perfect" performance review from a previous destination, the pilot goes through a preflight checklist every time without fail. This not only prepares the plane, but, more important, centers the pilot and prepares him for the upcoming performance.

Of all the high-achievers and business owners I've worked with, I've seen that, along with good habits, each has developed routines for accomplishing necessary daily disciplines. It's the only way any of us can predictably regulate our behavior. There simply isn't any way around it. A daily routine built on good habits and disciplines separates the most successful among us from everyone else. A routine is exceptionally powerful.

To create profitable and effective routines, you must first decide what behaviors and habits you want to implement. Take a moment to review your goals from Chapter 3, as well as the behaviors you want to add and subtract. Now it's your turn to be Jack Nicklaus and figure out your best pre-shot routine. Be intentional about what components belong. Once you establish, say, a morning routine, I want you to consider it cast in concrete until further notice. You get up. You do it—no argument. If someone or something interrupts you, start back at the beginning to anchor your foundation for the performance that follows.

Bookend Your Days

The key to becoming world-class in your endeavors is to build your performance around world-class routines. It can be difficult, even futile, to predict or control what will show up in the middle of your workday. But you can almost always control how your day starts and ends. I have routines for both. I'll share aspects of each here to give you some ideas and to help you better understand the power and importance of building your new behaviors into disciplined routines. Starting with my goals in mind, I designed my behaviors and routines accordingly. Perhaps in sharing some of what works for me, you'll identify strategies you'd like to try...

Rise & Shine

My morning routine is my Jack Nicklaus pre-shot preparation; it sets me up for the entire day. Because it happens every morning, it's locked in and I don't have to think about it. My iPhone alarm goes off at 5 a.m. (confession: sometimes, 5:30 a.m.) and I hit the Snooze button. Then I know I have eight minutes. Why eight? I have no idea, ask Steve Jobs; he programmed it. During those eight minutes I do three things: First, I think of all the things I'm grateful for. I know I need to attune my mind to abundance. The world looks, acts, and responds to you very differently when you start your day with a feeling and orientation of gratitude for that which you already have. Second, I do something that sounds a bit odd, but I send love to someone. The way to get love is to give it, and one thing I want more of is love. I give love by thinking of one person, anyone (it could be a friend, relative, co-worker, or someone I just met in the supermarket—it doesn't matter), and then I send them love by imagining all that I wish and hope for them. Some would call this a blessing or a prayer; I call it a mental love letter. Third, I think about my No. 1 goal and decide which three things I'm going to do on this day to move closer toward reaching it. For example, at the time of this writing, my No. 1 goal is to deepen the love and intimacy in my marriage. Each morning I plan three things I can do to make sure that my wife feels loved, respected, and beautiful.

When I get up, I put on a pot of coffee, and while it's brewing, I do a series of stretches for about ten minutes—something I picked up from Dr. Oz. If you've lifted weights your whole life as I have, you get stiff. I realized that the only way I was going to incorporate more stretching into my life was to make it a routine. I had to figure out where in my schedule I could stick it in—and while the coffee's brewing is as good a time as any.

Once I've stretched and poured my cup, I sit in my comfy leather recliner, set my iPhone for thirty minutes (no more, no less), and read something positive and instructional. When the alarm sounds, I take my most important project and work on it for an hour of completely focused and undistracted effort (notice I haven't opened e-mail yet). Then, every morning at 7 a.m., I have what I call my calibration appointment, a recurring appointment set in my calendar, where I take fifteen minutes to calibrate my day. This is where I brush over my top three one-year and five-year goals, my key quarterly objectives, and my top goal for the week and month. Then, for the most important part of the calibration appointment, I review (or set) my top three MVPs (Most Valuable Priorities) for that day, asking myself, "If I only did three things today, what are the actions that will produce the greatest results in moving me closer to my big goals?" Then, and only then, do I open e-mail and send out a flurry of tasks and delegations to get the rest of my team started on their day. I then quickly close down my e-mail and go to work on my MVPs.

The rest of the day can take a million different shapes, but as long as I go through my morning routine, a majority of the key disciplines I need to be practicing are taken care of, and I'm properly grounded and prepared to perform at a much higher level than if I started each day erratically—or worse, with a set of bad habits.

Sweet Dreams

In the evening I like to "cash out"—something I learned from waiting tables in my youth. Before we could go home, we had to cash out, meaning turn in all our receipts, credit card slips, and cash. Everything had to add up, or there was big trouble!

It's important to cash out your day's performance. Compared to your plan for the day, how did it go? What do you need to carry over to tomorrow's plan? What else needs to be added, based on what showed up throughout the day? What's no longer important and needs to be scratched out? Additionally, I like to log into my journal any new ideas, ah-has or insights I picked up throughout the day—this is how I've collected more than forty journals of incredible ideas, insights, and strategies. Finally, I like to read at least ten pages of an inspirational book before going to sleep. I know the mind continues to process the last information consumed before bedtime, so I want to focus my attention on something constructive and helpful in making progress with my goals and ambitions. That's it. All hell can break loose throughout the day, but because I control the bookends, I know I'm always going to start and finish strong.

Shake It Up

Every so often I like to interrupt my routines. Otherwise, life gets stale and I plateau. An easy example is working out with weights. When I work out the same way at the same time, doing the same repetitive movements week after week, my body stops showing compounded results. I get bored, lose my passion, and big Mo is a no-show. That's why it's important to mix it up, challenge yourself in new ways, and freshen up your experience!

Right now I'm working on adding more adventure into my life. I set weekly, monthly, and yearly goals to do something I wouldn't normally do. Most of the time it's nothing earth-shattering, but things such as eating different kinds of foods, taking a class, visiting a new destination, or joining a club to meet new people. This change of pace makes me feel alive, helps recapture my passion, and offers me opportunities for fresh perspectives.

Look at your routines. If something that used to energize you has become same-old/same-old, or is no longer generating powerful results, switch it up.

Getting into a Rhythm: Finding Your New Groove

Once your daily disciplines have become a routine, you want the succession of those steps to create a rhythm. When your disciplines and actions jibe into a regular weekly, monthly, quarterly, and yearly rhythm, it's like laying a welcome mat at the front door for Big Mo.

It's like the wheels of a steam locomotive. At a standstill, it takes very little to keep it from moving forward—a one-inch block of wood placed under the front wheel will do the job. It takes an incredible amount of steam to get the pistons to move and cause a series of connections that get the wheels to budge. It's a slow process. But once the train starts rolling, the wheels get into a rhythm. If the pressure remains consistent, the train gains momentum, and watch out! At 55 miles an hour, that train can crash through a five-foot, steel-reinforced concrete wall and keep on going. Envisioning your success as an unstoppable locomotive may help you stay enthusiastic about getting into your own rhythm. See Figure 9.

Fig. 9

When your disciplines and actions develop a rhythm, you welcome Big Mo.

Along with my daily rhythms, I also plan ahead. For instance, in looking again at my goal of deepening the love and intimacy of my marriage, I designed a weekly, monthly, and quarterly rhythm schedule. Doesn't sound too romantic, I know. But maybe you've noticed that, even when something's a high priority for you, if it isn't scheduled on your calendar, it often doesn't happen, right? Certainly not with the regularity you'll need to get into any kind of rhythm.

Here's how it works. Every Friday night is "date night," and Georgia and I go out or do something special together. At 6 p.m., an alarm goes off on both our iPhones, and no matter what we're doing, date night is on! Every Saturday is FD (Family Day)—which means NO working. Essentially sundown on Friday night until sunup on Sunday morning is time we devote to the marriage and family. If you don't create these boundaries, one day has a tendency to flow into the next. Unfortunately, the people who get shoved aside are often the most important.

Every Sunday night, also at 6 p.m., we have our RR (Relationship Review). This is a practice I picked up from relationship experts Linda and Richard Eyre during an interview I did with them for our October 2009 SUCCESS Audio Series. During this time, we discuss the previous week's wins, losses, as well as the adjustments we need to make in our relationship. We start the conversation by telling each other a few things we have appreciated about the other during the previous week—it's helpful to start with the good stuff. Then, using an idea I picked up from my interview with Jack Canfield, we ask each other, "On a scale of one to ten (ten being the best), how would you rate our relationship this week?" This gets the discussion of wins and losses flowing—oh, boy!

Then we discuss the adjustments that need to be made through this follow-up question: "What would it take to make your experience a ten?" By the end of the discussion, both of us feel heard and validated, and we have made our observations and wishes clear moving into the next week. This is an incredible process. I highly recommend it... if you dare!

Every month, Georgia and I also schedule something unique and memorable. Jim Rohn taught me that life is simply a collection of experiences; our goal should be to increase the frequency and the intensity of the good experiences. Once a month we try to do something that creates an experience that has some memorable intensity. It could be driving up to the mountains, going on an adventurous hike, driving up to Los Angeles to try a new fancy restaurant, going sailing in the bay— whatever. Something out of the ordinary that has a heightened experience and creates an indelible memory.

Once a quarter we plan a two- to three-day getaway. I like to do a quarterly review of all my goals and life patterns, and this is a great time to do a deeper check-in on how things are going in our relationship. Then we have our special travel vacation, plus our holiday traditions and our New Year's hike and goal-setting ritual. You can see that once all this is scheduled, you no longer have to think about what you need to be doing. Everything happens naturally. We've created a rhythm that gives us momentum.

Registering Your Rhythm

I want to share with you something I created for myself that helps me keep track of the rhythm of a new behavior. I call it my "Rhythm Register," and I think you'll find it extremely helpful.

Fig. 10

Weekly Rhythm Register [EXAMPLE]

Behavior/Action	Mon	Tues	Weds	Thurs	Fri	Sat	Sun	Achieved	Goal	Net
3 additional calls	X			X	X			3	5	<2>
3 additional presentations		X		X			·	2	3	<1>
30 minutes of cardio		X			X			2	3	<1>
Weight-training sessions	X	X		X				3	3	☺
Read 10 pages of a good book	X	X		X	X			4	5	<1>
Listen to 30 minutes of instructional audio	X	X	X			X		4	5	<1>
5 liters of water		X	X	X		X	X	5	7	<2>
Eat healthy breakfast	X	X		X		X		4	7	<3>
Dedicated time with kids	X			X		X		3	4	<1>
Date night with spouse					X			1	1	☺
Prayer/meditation time		X	X				X	3	5	<2>
Daily journaling	X		X		X	X	X	5	5	☺
							TOTAL	39	53	<14>

Commitment is doing the thing you said you were going to do
long after the mood you said it in has left you.

Date Range: _____

If you want to drink more water or take more steps each day or acknowledge your spouse more affectionately—whatever behavior you've decided you need to move toward your goal—you'll want to track it to make sure you're establishing a rhythm. See Figure 10. You can download a copy of the document for free at www.TheCompoundEffect.com/free. The Weekly Rhythm Register along with a weekly Plan, Do, Review and Improve process is an integral part of the *Living Your Best Year Ever* Achievement Management System™. Obtain your copy at www.SUCCESS.com/BestYearEver.

The Rhythms of Life

When people get started in a new endeavor, they almost always overdo it. Of course, I want you to feel excited about setting up a rhythm for success, but you need to find a program that you can absolutely, positively do in the long term without renegotiation. I don't want you thinking of the rhythms you can do for this week, month, or even the next ninety days; I want you to think about what you can do for the rest of your life. The Compound Effect—the positive results you want to experience in your life—will be the result of smart choices (and actions) repeated consistently over time. You win when you take the right steps day in and day out. But you set yourself up for failure by doing too much too soon.

A friend to the *SUCCESS* team (who will remain unnamed to protect the guilty) decided after seeing a picture I'd posted of him on Twitter that he was going to get in shape. This was a massive shift of lifestyle for him. On the job, he sits for at least a dozen hours a day, and he hates to exercise. Previously, he'd explained that he would find ways of avoiding using certain dishes or accessing files if it required him to squat and bend down to get them—that's how much of an aversion he had to physical activity. Still, he made a resolution to get in shape. He joined a gym, hired a personal trainer, and began working out two hours a day, five days a week. "Richard [let's call him]," I said, "that's a mistake. You will not be able to maintain that commitment and will eventually stop doing it. You're setting yourself up for failure." He pushed back, assuring me that he'd changed forever. Even his trainer had recommended the intense push. "I'm committed," he said. "I want to be able to see my abs."

"Richard, what's your real goal?" I asked him. I knew he wasn't gunning to be on the cover of *Men's Fitness*.

"I want to be trim; I want to be healthy," he told me. "Why?" I asked. "I want vitality. I want to be here long enough to see my kids have kids," he replied. These were his real, meaningful motivations; Richard wanted to be in it for the long haul. That meant he was signing on not for bikini season, but a long-term commitment to fitness.

"Okay," I said. "You've convinced me. But you're overdoing it. You're going to get two or three months down the road, and you're going to say, 'I don't have two hours to work out, so I guess I can't do it today.' That's going to happen to you over and over again. Working out five days a week will turn into two or three, and you'll get discouraged. Soon it will be over. I know you're really fired up right now, so let's do this: do your two hours a day, five days a week, for now [takes a lot of steam to get the wheels to budge from the inertia], but don't do it longer than sixty or ninety days. Then, I want you to scale it down to an hour or an hour and fifteen. You can still do your five days a week, but I would probably encourage you to go four. Do that another sixty to ninety days. Then I want you to consider an hour a day for a minimum of three days a week, four if you're feeling extra spry. That's the program I want you to work toward, because if you don't get into something you can maintain, you won't do it at all."

I really had to struggle to get Richard to comprehend this because, at that moment, he was all gung-ho. He thought he was going to be able to stick with his new routine for a lifetime. For someone who's never worked out to start working out two hours a day, five days a week, is a surefire dead end. You have to build a program that you can do for fifty years, not five weeks, or five months. It's okay if you go strong for a while, but you've got to see light at the end of the tunnel where you can start scaling it back. You can always find forty-five minutes to an hour a few times a week, but to find two hours, five days a week, to make your routine work, that'll never happen. Remember, consistency is a critical component of success.

The Power of Consistency

I've mentioned that if there's one discipline that gives me a competitive advantage, it's my ability to be consistent. Nothing kills Big Mo quicker and with more certainty than a lack of consistency. Even good, passionate, and ambitious people with good intentions can fall short when it comes to consistency. But it's a powerful tool you can use to launch the flight toward your goals.

Think of it like this: If you and I flew planes from Los Angeles to Manhattan, but you took off and landed in every state in between, while I flew straight through, even if you went five hundred miles per hour in the air and I only traveled at a rate of two hundred miles per hour, I'd still beat you by a big margin. The time and energy it takes for you to repeatedly stop and start and get back to momentum make your trip at least ten times as long. In fact, most likely you wouldn't even make it— you'd run out of fuel (energy, motivation, belief, will) at some point. It's far easier and requires a lot less energy to take off once and maintain a regular speed (even if slower than most everyone else) all along the way.

The Pump Well

When you start thinking about slacking off on your routines and rhythms, consider the massive cost of inconsistency. It is not the loss of the single action and tiny results it creates; it is the utter collapse and loss of momentum your entire progress will suffer.

Think of a hand-pumped water well, which uses a pipe to draw water up from the water table several feet underground. To get the water to the surface, you have to pump the well's lever to create the suction that brings the water above the ground and out of the spout. See Figure 11.

Fig. 11

Consistency is the key to achieving and maintaining momentum.

When most people start a new endeavor, they grab the lever and start pumping really hard. Just as Richard was with his plan to get fit, they're excited and committed... they pump and pump and pump, but after a few minutes (or a few weeks), when they don't see any water (results), they give up pumping the lever altogether. They don't realize how long it takes to create the vacuum needed to suck the water into the pipe and eventually out of the spout and into their bucket. Just like the merry-go-round, rocket ship, or steam engine breaking free of inertia, it takes time, massive energy, and consistency to pump water. Most people give up, but wise people continue to pump.

Those who persevere and continue to pump the lever will eventually get a few drops of water. This is when a lot of people say, "You've got to be kidding me! All this pumping, and for what—a few measly drops? Forget it!" Many people throw their hands up in defeat and quit, but wise people persist further.

And here's where the magic happens: If you continue to pump, it doesn't take long before you'll get a full and steady stream of water. You have your success! Now that the water is flowing, you no longer need to pump the lever as hard or as quickly. It becomes easy, actually. All you have to do to keep the pressure steady is to just pump the lever *consistently*. That's the Compound Effect.

Now, what happens if you let go of the lever for too long? The water falls back down into the ground, and you're back to square one. If you try to pump the lever easily and steadily, you won't get any water. Mo is gone; water is at the bottom. The only way to get it back up is to pump it really hard all over again. That's how most of us lead our lives, in fits and starts. We get a new business venture going, and then cut out on vacation. We start up a routine of making ten prospecting calls a day, strike a little gold, and then shift into neutral. We get hopped up about our new "date night" routine with our spouse, but in a few weeks, it's back to Netflix and microwave popcorn on the couch Friday nights. I see people buy a new book, sign up for a new program or seminar, and go like crazy for a couple of weeks or months. Then they stop and end up right back where they started. (Sound familiar?)

Miss only a couple weeks of anything—workouts at the gym, affectionate gestures toward your spouse, or the phone calls that are part of your prospecting routine—and you don't just lose the results those two weeks would have produced. If that's all you lost (which is what most people assume), not much damage would be done. But by slacking off for even a short time, you killed Mo. It's dead. And that's a tragedy.

Winning the race is all about pace. Be the tortoise. The

person who, given enough time, will beat virtually anybody in any competition as a result of positive habits and behaviors applied consistently. That'll put the mojo in your momentum. And keep it there!

Making the right choice, holding to right behaviors, practicing perfect habits, staying consistent, and keeping your momentum is easier said than done, especially in the dynamic, constantly changing, and always challenging world we share with billions of other people. In the next chapter I will discuss the many influences that (mostly unknowingly) can help or hinder your ability to succeed. These influences are pervasive, persuasive, and constant. Learn how to use them or you might end up losing because of them. Let me show you how…

Put the Compound Effect to Work for You

Summary Action Steps

> ↗ Build your bookend morning and evening routines. Design a predicable and fail-safe world-class routine schedule for your life.
>
> ↗ List three areas of life in which you are not consistent enough. What has this inconsistency cost you in life thus far? Make a declaration to stay steadfast in your new commitment to consistency.
>
> ↗ On your Rhythm Register, write down a half-dozen key behaviors relevant to your new goals. These should be behaviors you want to establish a rhythm with and eventually create momentum—Big Mo. Download the Rhythm Register at www.TheCompoundEffect.com/ free
>
> ↗ For a complete Achievement Management System™, including the Rhythm Register, obtain the *Living Your Best Year Ever* program at www.SUCCESS.com/ BestYearEver.

CHAPTER 5

INFLUENCES

Hopefully by now you understand exactly how important your choices are. Even those that seem insignificant, when compounded, can make an extreme impact on your life. We've also discussed the fact that you are 100 percent responsible for your life. You alone are responsible for the choices you make and the actions you take. That said, you must also realize your choices, behaviors, and habits are influenced by very powerful external forces. Most of us aren't aware of the subtle control these forces have on our lives. For you to sustain your positive trajectory toward your goals, you'll need to understand and govern these influences so they will support rather than derail your journey toward success. Everyone is affected by three kinds of influences: input (what you feed your mind), associations (the people with whom you spend time), and environment (your surroundings).

I. Input: Garbage In, Garbage Out

If you want your body to run at peak performance, you've got to be vigilant about consuming the highest-quality nutrients and avoiding tempting junk food. If you want your brain to perform at its peak, you've got to be even more vigilant about what you feed it. Are you feeding it news summaries or mind-numbing sitcoms? Are you reading the tabloids, or *SUCCESS*? Controlling the input has a direct and measurable impact on your productivity and outcomes.

Controlling what our brains consume is especially difficult because so much of what we take in is unconscious. Although it's true that we can eat without thinking, it's easier to pay attention to what we put in our bodies because food doesn't leap into our mouths. We need an extra level of vigilance to prevent our brains from absorbing irrelevant, counterproductive or downright destructive input. It's a never-ending battle to be selective and to stand guard against any information that can derail your creative potential.

Your brain is not designed to make you happy. Your brain has only one agenda in mind: survival. It is always watching for signs of "lack and attack." Your brain is programmed to seek out the negative—dwindling resources, destructive weather, whatever's out to hurt you. So when you switch on that radio on the way to work and get bombarded with all those reports about robberies, fires, attacks, the tanking economy, your brain lights up—it now will spend all day chewing over that feast of fear, worry, negativity. Same deal when you tune into the evening news after work. More bad news? Perfect! Your mind will stew on that all night long.

Left to its own devices, your mind will traffic in the negative, worrisome, and fearful all day and night. We can't change our DNA, but we *can* change our behavior. We can teach our minds to look beyond "lack and attack." How? We can protect and feed our mind. We can be disciplined and proactive about what we allow in.

To identify the influence that information and your environment has on you, complete the Input Influences sheet Sheet on page 171, or download at www.TheCompoundEffect.com/free

Don't Drink Dirty Water

You get in life what you create. Expectation drives the creative process. What do you expect? You expect whatever it is you're thinking about. Your thought process, the conversation in your head, is at the base of the results you create in life. So the question is, *What are you thinking about?* What is influencing and directing your thoughts? The answer: whatever you're allowing yourself to hear and see. This is the input you are feeding your brain. Period. See Figure 12.

Your mind is like an empty glass; it'll hold anything you put into it. You put in sensational news, salacious headlines, talk-show rants, and you're pouring dirty water into your glass. If you've got dark, dismal, worrisome water in your glass, everything you create will be filtered through that muddy mess, because that's what you'll be thinking about. Garbage

Fig. 12

Flush out the negative (dirty water) with positive, inspirational and supportive ideas (clean water).

in, garbage out. All that drive-time radio yak about murders, conspiracy, deaths, economy, and political battles drives your thinking process, which drives your expectations, which drives your creative output. That IS bad news. But just like a dirty glass, if you flush it with clean, clear water under the faucet long enough, eventually you'll end up with a glass of pure, clear water. What is that clear water? Positive, inspirational, and supportive input and ideas. Stories of aspiration, people who, despite challenges, are overcoming obstacles and achieving great things. Strategies of success, prosperity, health, love, and joy. Ideas to create more abundance, to grow, expand, and become more. Examples and stories of what's good, right, and possible in the world. That's why we work so hard at *SUCCESS* magazine. We want to provide you with those examples, those stories and the key take-aways you can use to improve your view of the world, yourself, and the results you create. That's also why I read something inspirational and instructional for thirty minutes in the morning and evening, and have personal-development CDs playing in my car. I'm flushing my glass and feeding my mind. Does this give me an edge over the guy who gets up and first thing reads the newspaper, listens to news radio on his commute to and from work, and watches the evening news before going to bed? You bet it does! And it can for you, too.

Step 1: Stand Guard

Unless you decide to hole up in a cave or on a desert island, you're going to get dirty water in your glass. It's going to be on billboards, on CNN while you're walking through the airport, on the screaming tabloid headlines at the checkout when you're buying groceries, etc. Even your friends, family members, and your own negative mental tapes can flood dirty water into your glass.

But that doesn't mean you can't take steps to limit your exposure to all that grime. Maybe you can't avoid the tabloids stacked up at the checkout register, but you can cancel your subscriptions. You can refuse to listen to the radio to and from work and instead put in an instructional and inspirational CD. You can turn off the evening news and talk to your loved ones instead. You can buy a DVR and record only those programs you feel are truly educational and life-affirming—and speed through the commercials aimed at making you feel inadequate or lacking unless you buy more crap.

I didn't really grow up with TV; I remember watching *Solid Gold* and *The A-Team* (remember them?), but television wasn't a big part of our family life. I managed somehow to thrive without it, and that's given me a clearer perspective when I watch an occasional program now. Sure, I'll laugh along with the sitcom, but afterward, I feel the same as if I ate fast food—bloated and malnourished. And I can't get over how commercials prey on our psychology, our fears, pains, needs, and weaknesses. If I walk through life thinking that I'm not enough just as I am—that I need to buy this, that, and the other thing to be okay—how can I expect to create amazing results?

It's estimated that Americans (twelve and older) spend 1,704 hours watching TV per year. That averages out to 4.7 HOURS per day. We're spending almost 30 percent of our waking hours watching TV. Almost thirty-three hours per week—more than one whole day each week! It's the equivalent of watching TV for two solid months out of every twelve! WOW! And people wonder why they can't get ahead in life?

Put Yourself on a Media Diet

The media thrives on taking us hostage. Ever been stuck on the freeway with traffic backed up for miles, making you late, wondering what the heck's holding everything up? Sure enough, when you finally get close, you see that nothing physical is blocking the flow of cars; the wreck clearly happened a while ago and has since been moved to the side of the freeway. The 3-mph crawl was caused by people rubbernecking! Now you're really irritated. But what happens when *your* car passes the wreck? You slow way down, take your eyes off the road in front of you, and crane your own neck!

Why do good, decent people want to see something tragic and grotesque? It's our genetic heritage, going back to our prehistoric sense of self-preservation. We can't help ourselves.

Even if we're adept at avoiding negativity, and have trained ourselves to be relentlessly positive, when it comes to sensationalism, our basic nature can't resist. Media masters understand that. They know your nature, in many ways better than you. The media has always used shocking and sensational headlines to draw attention. But today, instead of three news TV and radio networks, there are hundreds, running 24/7. Instead of a few newspapers, there are endless portals reaching us from our computers to our phones. The competition for your attention has never been bloodier, and the media jockeys continually up the ante in shock value. They find a dozen or so of the most heinous, scandalous, criminal, murderous, bleak, and horrid things that happen in the world each day, and parade them through our papers, news channels, and the Web over and over. Meanwhile, during that same twenty-four-hour period, millions of wonderful, beautiful, incredible things have happened. Yet we hear very little about them. In being wired to seek out the negative, we create the demand for more and more. How could the positive news stories ever hope to compete with those ratings or advertising dollars?

Let's go back to our freeway. Instead of a wreck on the side of the road, what if there was the most stunning, miraculous sunset you've ever seen? What would happen to the traffic then? I've seen this many times. It whizzes by at top speed.

The great danger of the media is that it gives us a very perverted view of the world. Because the focus and the repetition of messaging is on the negative, that's what our minds start believing. This warped and narrow view of what's not working has a severe influence on your creative potential. It can be crippling.

My Personal Junk Filter

I'll share what I do to safeguard my mind. But I warn you, I have a rigorous mental diet. You'll want to adjust to your own preferences, but this system has worked beautifully for me.

As you might guess, I don't watch or listen to *any* news and I don't read any newspapers or news magazines. Ninety-nine percent of all news has no bearing on my personal life or my personal goals, dreams, and ambitions anyway. I have set up a few RSS feeds identifying the news and industry updates that *do* pertain to my direct interests and goals. The news that's helpful to me gets plucked out of the fray so I don't have to get any mud slung into my glass of water. While most people wade through hours of irrelevant garbage that hampers their thinking and crushes their spirit, I get the most productive information I need when I need it, in less than fifteen minutes a day.

Step 2: Enroll in Drive-Time U

It's not enough to eliminate negative input. To move in a positive direction, you must flush out the bad and fill up on the good. My car won't move without two things: gasoline and an ever-present library of instructional CDs I listen to as I drive. The average American drives about twelve thousand miles a year. That's three hundred hours of flushing potential right there! Brian Tracy taught me the concept of turning my car into a mobile classroom. He explained to me that by listening to instructional CDs as I drive, I gain knowledge equivalent to two semesters of an advanced college degree—every year. Think about it; using the time you're currently wasting by listening to drive-time radio, you could obtain the equivalent of Ph.D. in leadership, sales success, wealth building, relationship excellence—or whatever course you choose. This commitment, in combination with your reading routine, separates you from the herd of average—one CD, DVD, or book at a time.

II. Associations: Who's Influencing You?

Birds of a feather flock together. The people with whom you habitually associate are called your "reference group." According to research by social psychologist Dr. David McClelland of Harvard, your "reference group" determines as much as 95 percent of your success or failure in life.

Who do you spend the most time with? Who are the people you most admire? Are those two groups of people exactly the same? If not, why not? Jim Rohn taught that we become the combined average of the five people we hang around the most. Rohn would say we could tell the quality of our health, attitude, and income by looking at the people around us. The people with whom we spend our time determine what conversations dominate our attention, and to which attitudes and opinions we are regularly exposed. Eventually, we start to eat what they eat, talk like they talk, read what they read, think like they think, watch what they watch, treat people how they treat them, even dress like they dress. The funny thing is, more often than not, we are completely unaware of the similarities between us and our circle of five.

How are we not aware? Because your associations don't shove you in a direction; they nudge you ever so slightly over time. Their influence is so subtle that it's like being on an inner tube out in the ocean, feeling like you're floating in place, until you look up and realize the gentle current has pushed you a half mile down the shore.

Think of your friends who order greasy appetizers or a cocktail before dinner, and that's their routine. Hang out with them enough, and you'll find yourself grabbing for cheese nachos and potato skins, and joining them for that extra beer or glass of wine, matching their pace. Meanwhile, your other friends order healthy food and talk about the inspiring books they're reading and their ambitions in their businesses, and you begin to assimilate their behaviors and habits. You read and talk about what they talk about, you see the movies they're excited about, and you go to the places they recommend. The influence your friends have over you is subtle and can be positive or negative; either way, the impact is incredibly powerful. Watch out! You cannot hang out with negative people and expect to live a positive life.

So, what *is* the combined average income, health, or attitudes of the five people you spend most of your time with? Does the answer frighten you? If so, the best way to increase your potential for whatever traits you desire is to spend the majority of your time with people who already possess those traits. You will then see the power of influence work for you, rather than against you. The behaviors and attitudes which helped them acquire the success you admire will begin to become part of your daily routine. Hang around them long enough, and you're likely to realize similar successful outcomes in your life.

If you haven't already, jot down the names of those five people you hang around the most. Also write down their main characteristics, both positive and negative. It doesn't matter who they are. It could be your spouse, your brother, your neighbor, or your assistant. Now, average them out. What's their average health, and bank balance? What's their average relationship like? As you look at your results, ask yourself, "Is this list okay for me? Is this where I want to go?"

It's time to reappraise and reprioritize the people you spend time with. These relationships can nurture you, starve you, or keep you stuck. Now that you've started to carefully consider with whom you spend your time, let's go a little deeper. As Jim Rohn taught me, it's powerful to evaluate and shift your associations into three categories: dissociations, limited associations, and expanded associations.

 To evaluate your current associations, complete the Association Evaluator sheet on page 172, or download at www.TheCompoundEffect.com/free

Dissociations

You guard against the influences your children are exposed to, and the people they hang around. You are aware of the influence these people could have on your children and the choices they might make as a result. I believe this same principle should apply to you! You already know this: There are some people you might need to break away from. Completely. This might not be an easy step to take, but it's essential. You have to make the hard choice not to let certain negative influences affect you anymore. Determine the quality of life you want to have, and then surround yourself with the people who represent and support that vision.

I'm constantly weeding out of my life people who refuse to grow and live positively. Growing and changing your associations is a lifelong process. Some people might say I'm too rigorous about it, but I'd like to be more so. I had a business relationship with someone I really liked, but when the economy got difficult, most of his conversation was focused on how horrible things were, how much his company was feeling the hit, and how hard it was out there. I said, "Man, you've got to stop working on your presentation about how bad life is. I can hear you collecting all the data points to reinforce your beliefs." He persisted in seeing everything as more dour and hopeless than it was, and I decided we had no business doing business together.

When you make the tough decision to put up boundaries between you and people who drag you down, realize that they'll fight you—especially those closest to you. Your decision to live a more positive, goal-oriented life will be a mirror to their own poor choices. You will make them uncomfortable and they will attempt to pull you back down to their level. Their resistance doesn't mean they don't love you or want the best for you—it's actually not about you at all. It's about their fear and their guilt about their own poor choices and lack of discipline. Just know that breaking away won't be easy.

Limited Associations

There are some people you can spend three hours with, but not three days. Others you can spend three minutes with, but not three hours. Always remember that the influence of associations is both powerful and subtle. The person you're walking with can determine whether you slow your pace or quicken it, literally and figuratively. Similarly, you can't help but be touched by the dominant attitudes, actions and behaviors of the people with whom you spend time.

Decide how much you can "afford" to be influenced, based on how those people represent themselves. This is difficult, I know. I have had to do this on several occasions, even with close family members. I WILL NOT, however, allow someone else's actions or attitudes to have a dampening influence on me.

I've got a neighbor who's a three-minute friend. For three minutes, we have a great chit-chat, but we wouldn't mesh for three hours. I can hang out with an old high-school friend for three hours, but he's not a three-day guy. And, then there are some people I can hang around for a few days, but wouldn't go on an extended vacation with. Take a look at your relationships and make sure you're not spending three hours with a three-minute person.

Expanded Associations

We've just talked about weeding out negative influencers. While you're doing that, you'll also want to *reach* out. Identify people who have positive qualities in the areas of life where you want to improve—people with the financial and business success you desire, the parenting skills you want, the relationships you yearn for, the lifestyle you love. And then spend more time with them. Join organizations and businesses and health clubs where these people gather and make friends. Ahead, you'll see how I even used to drive to a different town to spend quality time—with fortuitous results.

I rave about Jim Rohn throughout this book because, aside from my father, Jim remains my foremost mentor and influencer. My relationship with Jim perfectly exemplifies an expanded association. While I got to share a few private meals and spend a little time with him during our interviews and backstage before events, most of my time with Jim was spent listening to him in my car or reading his words in my living room. I have spent more than a thousand hours getting direct instruction from Jim, and 99 percent of that was through books and audio programs. What's exciting about that is, no matter where you are in your life—maybe busy at home with small children or caretaking aging parents, working long hours with people with whom you have little in common, or living out in the country far from the nearest office building—you, too, can have almost any mentor you want, if he or she has gathered their best thoughts, stories, and ideas into books, CDs, DVDs, and podcasts. You have an unlimited bounty from which to draw. Take advantage of it.

If you want to have a better, deeper, more meaningful relationship, ask yourself, "Who has the type of relationship I want? How can I spend (more) time with that person? Who can I meet who can positively influence me?" Let their glow rub off on you. Befriend the person you think is the biggest, baddest, most successful person in your field. What do they read? Where do they go for lunch? How can that association influence you? You can build these expanded associations by joining networking groups, Toastmasters, and similar organizations. Find the charity organizations, symphonies, country clubs, where the people you want to emulate gather.

Find a Peak-Performance Partner

Another way to increase your exposure to expanded associations is by teaming up with a peak performance partner, someone as equally committed to study and personal growth as you. This person should be someone you trust, someone bold enough to tell you what they really think about you, your attitudes, and performance. It could be that this person is a longtime friend, but he or she may be someone who doesn't know you well at all. The point is to get (and give) an unbiased, honest, outside perspective.

My current "accountability partner" is my good friend Landon Taylor. As I mentioned before, we have a thirty-minute call every Friday to discuss our weekly wins, losses, fixes, "ah-has," and where we are on our growth plans. The anticipation of the call and knowing I have to be accountable to Landon keeps me extra committed throughout the week.

I make a record of Landon's losses or any feedback he needs and make sure to ask him about it the next week. He does the same for me. That way we hold each other accountable. He might say, "Okay, you screwed up here last week and admitted it and committed to change. What did you do about that this week?" Life is life. We're both busy executives, but it's amazing to me that we actually end up doing this every week without fail. It's not easy. Sometimes I'll be flying through my day and think, "Oh, crud! I have to do this." But often in the middle of the call, I'll think, "I'm so glad we're having this conversation!" Even in preparing for it, and thinking of my big wins and losses for the week, I learn about myself. This week I told Landon, "You know, I'm in the middle of so many things. I'm writing my book. I'm having a lot of realizations, and so many ah-has, but not one thing that's really compelling." He said, "Let this be the last week that you don't come to the table with an ah-ha." Gulp. "Don't shortchange me," he said. Point taken. In reality, I was shortchanging myself by not identifying one thing memorable enough to share.

I have a serious challenge for you if you're up for it. Want real feedback? Find people who care enough about you to be brutally honest with you. Ask them these questions: "How do I show up to you? What do you think my strengths are? In what areas do you think I can improve? Where do you think I sabotage myself? What's one thing I can stop doing that would benefit me the most? What's the one thing I should start doing?"

Invest in Mentorship

Paul J. Meyer is another man who served as a mentor to me. Paul passed away in 2009 at age eighty-one. Whenever I thought I was really doing things, really playing at a high level, I'd get around Paul—he was my reality check. What he did before lunch was mind-boggling to me. I got to spend a lot of time with him; Paul bought one of my companies, and then I did a turnaround for one of his companies. He was a very powerful spirit in my life.

After spending a couple of hours with Paul, hearing about all his plans and ventures and activities, my head would spin. Just trying to make sense of all he had going on exhausted me. After time with Paul, I'd want to go take a nap! But my association with him raised my game. His walking pace was my running pace. It expanded my ideas about how big I could play and how ambitious I could be. You have to get around people like that!

You're never too good for a mentor. During my interview with Harvey Mackay, he told me, "I have had twenty coaches, if you can believe it. I have a speech coach, I have a writing coach, I have a humor coach, I've got a language coach, and on and on." I have always found it interesting that the most successful people, the truly top performers, are the ones willing to hire and pay for the best coaches and trainers there are. It pays to invest in your improved performance.

Finding and engaging a mentor doesn't need to be a mysterious or intimidating process either. When I sat down with Ken Blanchard, he explained the simplicity of engaging a mentor (*SUCCESS*, January 2010): "The first thing you want to remember with a mentor is that it doesn't need to take a lot of their time. The best advice I've ever gotten is in short clips, having lunch or breakfast with somebody, just telling them what I'm working on and asking their advice and all. You will be amazed how successful businesspeople are willing to be mentors to people when it's not taking a lot of time." John Wooden reinforces the point that others desire to be mentors (*SUCCESS*, September 2008): "Mentoring is your true legacy. It is the greatest inheritance you can give to others. And it should never end. It is why you get up every day. To teach and be taught." He went on to explain that mentorship is also a two-way street. "An individual needs to be open to being mentored. It is our responsibility to be willing to allow our lives and our minds to be touched, molded, and strengthened by the people who surround us."

Develop Your Own Personal Board of Advisors

As part of my plan to be wiser, more strategic, and operate more effectively, as well as expand the time and interaction I have with high-minded leaders, I've been developing a board of advisors in my personal life.

I've hand-selected a dozen people because of their areas of expertise, creative thinking ability, and/or my great respect for who they are. Once a week I reach out to a few of them and solicit ideas, run thoughts by them, and ask for feedback and input. Having started this process, I can tell you the benefits I've already received have been profound—far more than I anticipated! It's surprising the genius people are willing to share when you show sincere interest.

Who should be on your personal board of advisors? Seek out positive people who have achieved the success you want to create in your own life. Remember the adage: "Never ask advice of someone with whom you wouldn't want to trade places."

III. Environment: Changing Your View Changes Your Perspective

When I was in real estate, working in the East Bay of San Francisco, I lived and worked within a very limited demographic. I saw the same kinds of people operating at the same level over and over. I knew that I needed to find an elevated circle of associations in order to go where I wanted to go.

I started driving across the bay to one of the richest and most beautiful spots on the planet, Tiburon in Marin County, north of San Francisco. If you've ever been to Monaco, that's what Tiburon looks like, but far quainter. It's a spectacular spot. I would go to a delightful seafood restaurant, Sam's on the Wharf. The food was great, but more importantly, the restaurant was popular with the area's more affluent residents.

Aside from going to Sam's to expand my associations, I'd also sit on the wharf and look up at the hillside. I was mesmerized by the multimillion-dollar houses that hung off the cliffs. One in particular always caught my eye—a blue, four-story home with an elevator and a whale lightning rod at the top. *What would be the perfect house?* I used to ask myself all the time. *If someone could just give me one of them, which one would I pick?* The answer was always the same—this beautiful blue one. It was in the perfect spot with a bright vista, the best of the bunch.

On my way home from brunch one morning, I saw an open house sign and thought it'd be fun to check it out. One sign led to another as I followed them zigzagging up the cliffs along the narrow streets. I finally reached the top of the hill and found the advertised home. As I entered and walked up to a spectacular bay window, the world opened up in front of me—the peninsula tip of Tiburon, Angel Island across the Bay, Berkeley and the East Bay, the Bay Bridge, and the entire San Francisco skyline over to the Golden Gate Bridge in a 300-degree expanse. I walked out onto the balcony and looked around. Suddenly I realized that this was the very house I'd been looking at for years! This was the blue house! I signed the contract on the spot. My dream house was now mine!

I can't really say that I met anybody at Sam's who changed my life. However, that environment had a powerful effect on me. Seeing those homes up on the cliffs fueled my ambition and expanded my dreams. I ended up working harder than I ever thought possible to make those dreams come true—and they did!

The dream in your heart may be bigger than the environment in which you find yourself. Sometimes you have to get out of that environment to see that dream fulfilled. It's like planting an oak sapling in a pot. Once it becomes rootbound, its growth is limited. It needs a great space to become a mighty oak. So do you.

When I talk about your environment, I'm not just referring to where you live. I'm referring to whatever surrounds you. Creating a positive environment to support your success means clearing out all the clutter in your life. Not just the physical clutter that makes it hard for you to work productively and efficiently (although that's important too!), but also the psychic clutter of whatever around you isn't working, whatever's broken, whatever makes you cringe. Each and every incomplete thing in your life exerts a draining force on you, sucking the energy of accomplishment and success out of you as surely as a vampire stealing your blood. Every incomplete promise, commitment, and agreement saps your strength because it blocks your momentum and inhibits your ability to move forward. Incomplete tasks keep calling you back to the past to take care of them. So think about what you can complete today.

Additionally, when you're creating an environment to support your goals, remember that you get in life what you *tolerate*. This is true in every area of your life—particularly within your relationships with family, friends, and colleagues. What you have decided to tolerate is also reflected in the situations and circumstances of your life right now. Put another way, *you will get in life what you accept and expect you are worthy of.*

If you tolerate disrespect, you will be disrespected. If you tolerate people being late and making you wait, people will show up late for you. If you tolerate being underpaid and overworked, that will continue for you. If you tolerate your body being overweight, tired, and perpetually sick, it will be.

It's amazing how life will organize around the standards you set for yourself. Some people think they're the victims of other people's behavior, but in actuality, we have control over how people treat us. Protect your emotional, mental, and physical space so you can live with peace, rather than in the chaos and stress the world will hurl upon you.

If you want to foster a disciplined routine of rhythms and consistency so that Big Mo not only pays a visit to your house but moves in, you have to be sure your environment is welcoming and supportive of your becoming, doing, and performing at world-class levels.

While we're on the topic of world-class, in the next chapter, I want to help you take everything you've learned thus far and give you the secret to now accelerating your results. Getting greater results with only a little more effort may feel a little like cheating... like an unfair advantage. But who said life was fair?

Put the Compound Effect to Work for You

Summary Action Steps

↗ Identify the influence the input of media and information is having on your life. Determine what input you need to protect your glass (mind) from and how you are going to keep your glass (mind) regularly flushed with positive, uplifting, and supportive input. Download the Input Influence sheet at www.TheCompoundEffect.com/free

↗ Evaluate your current associations. Who might you need to further limit your association? Who might you need to completely dissociate from? Strategize ways you will expand your associations. Download the Association Assessment sheet at www.TheCompoundEffect.com/free

↗ Pick a peak-performance partner. Decide when, how regularly, and what you will hold each other accountable to, and what ideas you will expect the other to bring to each conversation.

↗ Identify the three areas of your life you are most focused on improving. Find and engage a mentor in each of those areas. Your mentors could be people who have accomplished what you wish to and with whom you have brief conversations, or they could be experts who have written down their ideas in books or recorded their ideas on CDs.

CHAPTER 6

ACCELERATION

When I lived in La Jolla, California, for exercise and a test of will, I would regularly ride my bike two miles straight up Mount Soledad. There are very few things you can do voluntarily that cause more pain and suffering than riding a bike up a steep mountain without stopping. There is a point at which you "hit the wall" and come face to face with your true inner character. Suddenly, all the projections and ideas you had about yourself are stripped away and you're left with the naked truth. Your mind starts inventing all sorts of convenient alibis on why it's okay to stop. It is then when you're faced with one of life's greatest questions: Do you push through the pain and continue on, or will you crack like a walnut and give up?

Lance Armstrong was the *SUCCESS* cover feature in June 2009. I remember watching Lance during his first Tour de France victory. The Tour had entered the grueling mountain stages of the race. The other riders dismissed Lance, because he had never been a renowned climber. During the third mountain ascent through freezing rains, mist, and then hail, Lance got separated from his team. He was left fighting the top climbers in the world, alone. On the final ascent, eighteen miles straight up into Sestriere, after five and a half hours climbing mountains, every rider was suffering. Each needed to search the depths of his stamina and self-definition—could they endure? It became a test of who could best survive the hardships and find the strength to keep going—who would crack and who wouldn't.

With five miles to go, Lance was thirty-two seconds behind the leaders, an eternity while climbing a mountain on a bike. During a curve, Lance stood up and surged ahead until he caught the two leaders—both established world-class climbers. Having expended almost everything he had in him, Lance then launched an attack and gained several lengths on the leaders. He later said in his book *It's Not About the Bike: My Journey Back to Life* (Putnam, 2000), "When you open a gap and your competitors don't respond, it tells you something. They're hurting. And when they're hurting, that is when you take them." Completely exhausted, struggling to breathe, his legs and arms burning with fatigue, Lance kept pounding the pedals. Some tried, but no one could catch him, they just didn't have it in them. At the finish line, with fists pumping in the air, the unexpected contender won the stage race and ultimately the Tour de France.

In this chapter I want to talk to you about those moments of truth and how the Compound Effect can help you break through to new and greater levels of success—faster than you imagined possible. When you've prepared, practiced, studied, and consistently put in the required effort, sooner or later you'll be presented with your own moment of truth. In that moment, you will define who you are and who you are becoming. It is in those moments where growth and improvement live—when we either step forward or shrink back, when we climb to the top of the podium and seize the medal or we continue to applaud sullenly from the crowd for others' victories.

We'll also look at how you can consistently deliver more than people expect, compounding your good fortune even further.

Moments of Truth

"There is a point in every race when a rider encounters his real opponent and understands that it's himself," writes Lance in his autobiography. "In my most painful moments on the bike, I am at my most curious, and I wonder each and every time how I will respond. Will I discover my innermost weakness, or will I seek out my innermost strength?"

When I was in real estate, I hit the wall several times a day. While driving to an expired listing property, after just getting pummeled by the last prospect, I'd start conjuring up all sorts of excuses to skip the sales call and head back to the office. While out canvassing a neighborhood, dogs would snarl at me or it looked like it might start to rain. I'd be in the midst of "money time" (5 to 9 p.m., cold-calling) and frequently get chewed out for interrupting someone's dinner or favorite TV show. I was sure I needed to take a break to go to the bathroom or get a glass of water. But instead of quitting, every time I hit one of those mental and emotional walls, I recognized that my competitors were facing the same challenges. I knew this was another moment that, if I kept going, I would be strides ahead of them. These were the defining moments of success and progress. It wasn't difficult, painful, or challenging when I was just running with the herd, just keeping up, but not really getting ahead. It's not getting to the wall that counts; it's what you do *after* you hit it.

Lou Holtz, the famous football coach, knew it was what you did after you did your best that created victories. In one game his team was down 42-0 at halftime. During the half-time break, Lou showed his team a dramatic highlight reel of second efforts to block, tackle, and recover the ball. He then told the players that they were not on his team because they could give their all on every play; every player on every team does that. He said they were on *his* team because of their ability to make that critical extra effort on each play. It's the extra effort after you have done your best that is the difference maker. His team went on to win the game in the second half. That is how you win.

Muhammad Ali was one of the greatest fighters of all time, not only because of his speed and agility, but also because of his strategy. On October 30, 1974, Ali regained his heavyweight championship, besting George Foreman in one of the biggest upsets in boxing history in the "Rumble in the Jungle." Almost no one, not even Ali's longtime supporter Howard Cosell, believed the former champion had a chance of winning. Both Joe Frazier and Ken Norton had beaten Ali previously, and George Foreman had knocked both of them out in only the second round. Ali's strategy? To take advantage of the younger champion's weakness—his lack of staying power. Ali knew if he could get Foreman to his wall, he could then take the advantage. This is when Ali came up with the tactic later termed "Rope-a-Dope." Ali would lean on the ropes, shielding his face, while Foreman threw hundreds of punches over seven rounds. By the eighth round, Foreman was exhausted; he was at his wall. It was then that Ali dropped Foreman with a combination at center ring.

Hitting the wall isn't an obstacle; it's an opportunity. During Lance Armstrong's second attempt at winning the Tour de France, it was once again time to head into the mountains. The first big climb would be where Lance had experienced a devastating crash on a wet, spring day earlier that same year. The crash left him with a concussion and a broken vertebra. Now it was raining yet again. Instead of being concerned or hesitant, he said, "This is perfect attacking weather, mainly because I know the others don't like it. I believe that nobody in the world is better at suffering. It's a good day for me." He was right. Lance brought home his second v ictory.

When conditions are great, things are easy, there aren't any distractions, no one is interrupting, temptations aren't luring, and nothing is disturbing your stride; that too is when most everyone else does great. It's not until situations are difficult, when problems come up and temptation is great, that you get to prove your worthiness for progress. As Jim Rohn would say, "Don't wish it were easier; wish you were better."

When you hit the wall in your disciplines, routines, rhythms, and consistency, realize that's when you are separating yourself from your old self, scaling that wall, and finding your new powerful, triumphant, and victorious self.

Multiplying Your Results

I have an exciting opportunity for you. We've talked about how the simple disciplines and behaviors will compound over time, delivering amazingly powerful results for you. What if you could speed up the process and multiply your results? Would you be interested? I want to show you how just a little bit more effort can add exponentially to your outcomes.

Let's say you're weight training and your program calls for you to do twelve repetitions of a certain weight. Now, if you do the twelve, you're fulfilling the expectation of your program. Great job. Stay consistent, and ultimately, you will see this discipline compound into powerful results for you. Yet, if you get to twelve, even if you've hit your max, and you push out another three to five reps, your impact on that set will be multiplied several times. You won't just add a few reps to the aggregate of your workout. No. Those reps done after you hit your max will *multiply* your results. You've just pushed through the wall of your max. The previous reps just got you there. The real growth happens with what you do *after* you're at the wall.

Arnold Schwarzenegger made famous a weight training method called "The Cheating Principle." Arnold was a stickler for perfect technique. He contended that once you reached your maximum number of lifts in perfect form, adjusting your wrists or leaning back to recruit other muscles to assist the working muscles (cheating a little) would allow you to do five or six more reps, which would significantly improve the results of that set. (You can also achieve this by having a workout partner who assists the last few reps you couldn't have done on your own.)

If you're a runner, you know the experience. You get to the goal you set for yourself that day, and you're feeling the burn, you're at your wall, but you go a little farther, a little longer.

This "little longer" is really a massive expansion of your limits. You have multiplied the results of that single run.

Take the magic penny we talked about in Chapter 1, the one that doubles in value each day, showing you the result of small compounded actions. If you just doubled that penny one extra time per week during those same thirty-one days, the compounded penny would result in $171 million instead of $10 million. Again, just extra effort in four days and the result was many times greater. That is how the math of doing just a little bit more than expected works.

Viewing yourself as your toughest competitor is one of the best ways to multiply your results. Go above and beyond when you hit the wall. Another way to multiply your results is pushing past what *other* people expect of you—doing more than "enough."

Beat the Expectations

Oprah is famous for using this principle—blasting beyond anyone's expectations with her generosity and ability to live and work in a BIG way. Do you remember how she launched her nineteenth season in September 2004? When it comes to Oprah, we know to expect some fanfare… but she blew everyone away. That season opener was all the media or anyone else talked about for days afterward.

Let's go back in time for a minute…. The audience members were selected because their friends and family members had written in saying each of them desperately needed a new car. Oprah opened the show by calling eleven people to the stage. She gave every one of them a car—a 2005 Pontiac G6. Then the real surprise: She surpassed everyone's expectations when she distributed gift boxes to the rest of the audience saying one of the boxes contained a key to the twelfth car. But when the audience members opened their boxes, every one of them had a set of keys. She screamed, "Everybody gets a car! Everybody gets a car!"

While this might be her most famous example, Oprah continues to go beyond our expectations in most everything she does. In other segments, Oprah surprised a twenty-year-old girl who had spent years in foster care and homeless shelters with a four-year college scholarship, a makeover and $10,000 in clothes. And, she gave a family with eight foster children who were going to be kicked out of their house $130,000 to pay for and repair their home.

Now you might be saying, yeah, but she's Oprah, of course she can do those things. But the truth is there are plenty of others in Oprah's position—with the finances and the fame—who could do those things, but never venture into the realm of extraordinary. Oprah does. That's what makes her Oprah. Take a lesson from her. You can do more than expected in every aspect of your life.

When it was time to propose to my wife, Georgia, I could have done what was expected and met with her father to ask for his daughter's hand in marriage. Instead, I decided to pay great respect to her father by preparing my speech in Portuguese (I got Georgia's sister to translate what I wanted to say). He understood English well enough, but wasn't entirely comfortable with it. All the way up to Los Angeles from San Diego, I rehearsed the words. I walked through the door carrying flowers and treats and asked her dad to join us in the living room. I then delivered my memorized speech. Thankfully, he said, "Yes!"

But I didn't stop there. On the way back, and over the next couple of days, I called each one of her FIVE brothers and also asked for their blessing to join the family. Some were easy to convince, others proceeded to have me "earn it." The point is, she told me later that one of the most special aspects about how I proposed was how I had honored her dad and how I had called every one of her brothers (and had her sister teach me Portuguese). That made the act extra special. The result of that extra effort paid off exponentially.

Stuart Johnson owns the parent company to *SUCCESS*, VideoPlus L.P. Stuart put a lot of money and a twenty-two-year reputation on the line when he decided to acquire *SUCCESS* magazine, SUCCESS.com and the other properties of SUCCESS Media. During one of the most challenging economies in recent history, and as print publishing was being seen as unfavorable, the move in itself was bold and audacious, but then he did even more than could be expected. While the new business enterprise was still finding its legs (translation: still operating in the red), and his primary business was taking a couple steps backward like the rest of the world during the economic tsunami of 2008 and 2009, Stuart launched a nonprofit foundation dedicated to kids. If he was going to make a commitment to helping teach the fundamentals of personal development to the world, he wanted to be especially sure that information would reach teenagers. So he launched the SUCCESS Foundation (www.SUCCESSFoundation.org). He had the fundamental principles of personal achievement compiled into a book called *SUCCESS for Teens* and is distributing it for *free* through responsible partners and nonprofit organizations to help nurture young minds.

Stuart personally funded the administration and management of the SUCCESS Foundation, and for the first year, with the help of a few good friends, he funded the distribution of more than 1 million books. Today, that number is far greater and growing! Now, Stuart was already in for a heavy investment and big risk without the burdens of funding the new foundation. But the additional contribution and dedication to the foundation multiplied the statement of his commitment several-fold to potential partners, the press, his peers, and his own staff. He was doing far more than expected—and it spoke volumes.

Where in life can you do more than expected when you hit the wall? Or where can you go for "WOW"? It doesn't take a lot more effort, but the little extra multiplies your results many times over. Whether you're making calls, serving customers, recognizing your team, acknowledging your spouse, going for a run, bench pressing, planning a date night, sharing time with your kids, whatever… what's the little extra you can do that exceeds expectations and accelerates your results?

Do the Unexpected

I'm a contrarian by nature, I know. Tell me what everyone else does, what's the consensus and what's popular, and I will typically do the opposite. If everyone is zigging, I'm gonna zag. To me, what's popular is average, it's what's common. Common things deliver common results. The most popular restaurant is McDonald's, the most popular drink is Coca-Cola, the most popular beer is Budweiser, the most popular wine is Franzia (yeah, the stuff that comes in a box!). Consume those "popular" things, and you'll be part of the common, average pack. But that's ordinary. There's nothing wrong with ordinary. I just prefer to shoot for extraordinary.

For instance, everyone sends Christmas cards. But, since *everyone* does, it doesn't really have much emotional impact, in my opinion. So I choose to send Thanksgiving cards instead. How many Thanksgiving cards do you get? Exactly. It makes a statement. And instead of bulk-printed, computer-generated "best wishes" cards, I handwrite personal sentiments expressing how grateful I am for my relationship with that person and what he or she means to me—same effort, but a much greater impact.

Richard Branson built his career on doing the unexpected. I love to watch him launch a new company. Each stunt is bolder, scarier, and more unexpected than the last. Whether it's flying a hot air balloon around the globe or driving a tank down Fifth Avenue in New York to introduce Virgin Cola to the United States, Richard always delivers the unexpected. He could get by with the expected press release, a press conference or two, and some swanky party, and call it a day, but instead he goes for the astonishing. He probably spends as much as (and sometimes even less than) other companies do to launch a product; he just does it in unexpected style. The wow-factor makes a statement and multiplies the impact of his efforts.

More often than not, the extra effort doesn't cost that much more money or energy. When I was selling real estate, everyone else would call on expired listings when they came up. Instead, I got in my car and showed up on their doorstep and hand-delivered a "SOLD" sign. "Take this," I'd say when they'd open the door. "You'll need it if you hire me to take over this listing." For the price it took to keep my gas tank full, I immediately and exponentially increased my chance of getting the listing.

Recently Alex, a friend of mine, was up for a big job. He lives in California and the job was in Boston. He was one of a final twelve candidates. They were going to interview local candidates in person and those out of the area via video conferencing. He called me, asking if I knew how to facilitate a Web camera video conference.

"How badly do you want this job?" I asked him.

"It's my dream job," Alex told me. "It's everything I've spent forty-five years preparing to do."

"Then get on a plane and show up in person." I said.

"No need," Alex said, "They're flying in the final three for a last interview."

"Listen," I told him. "If you want to be in that final three, you should separate yourself by doing the unexpected. Fly across the country on a moment's notice and show up in person. That's how you make a statement."

If I set my sights on something, I'm going to ensure success by going all in and all out. I launch what I call "shock and awe" campaigns. During this same job hunt I suggested Alex pull out all the stops—attack from every possible front and do it relentlessly.

"Research all the decision makers," I told him. "Find out their interests, hobbies, kids' hobbies, spouses' hobbies, neighbors' hobbies, etc. Send them books, articles, gifts, and other resources that you think they might like. 'Is this over the top?' Heck yes, that's the point. They'll know you're trying to butter them up, but they'll appreciate your gumption and creativity—you'll certainly get their attention and most likely, their respect." Then I continued: "Research all the people in the organization. Take that list and run it by your entire network to see if they know anyone who might know someone in this organization. Search every name against your LinkedIn database. Find a few people to connect with. Talk with them and ask them to put in a good word for you. Send them gifts, notes, and other things, and ask them to hand-deliver these things to the decision makers. Phone, e-mail, fax, text, tweet, Facebook, etc., them during the process. Could this be overly aggressive? Heck, yes! But I have found that you may lose one out of five for being too aggressive, but you get the other four!"

By the way, Alex did not take my advice, and he did not get the job. He didn't even get to be in the final three. I can unequivocally say he was a far better choice than the person the organization hired, but Alex failed to make an impression, and it cost him his dream job.

I'm on the board of a company that needed a congressman to sign off on a piece of legislation that affected whether this company could move forward on an important project. This guy wasn't budging, not because of the actual issue, but because of a political axe he was grinding against others who publicly favored the issue. Instead of making any more futile appeals to sway him, I suggested we go above his head and talk to his boss—his wife. We went through our network until one person led us to someone who was friends with his wife. We then waited for her outside following a church service she attended, and had her friend introduce us. We explained our important case and cause, which was to build an after-school facility in an impoverished neighborhood that would affect the lives of hundreds of children if her husband would support it. Needless to say, he signed on by Tuesday that following week and the company got its project.

In our attention-deficit, propaganda-saturated society, sometimes doing the unexpected is required to get your voice heard. If you have a cause or ideal worthy of attention, do what it takes, even the unexpected, to make your case heard. Add a little audacity to your repertoire.

Do Better Than Expected

Invisible Children (www.InvisibleChildren.com), another nonprofit for which I'm a board member, helps rescue and recuperate children who have been abducted and made soldiers in northern Uganda and the Congo. To gain awareness for their cause, they staged a hundred-city event called "The Rescue," where more than eight hundred thousand young people camped outside until prominent leaders of the community came to "rescue them," thus gaining their attention and support. After four days, all but one city had been rescued, having people like U.S. Sens. Ted Kennedy and John Kerry, Val Kilmer, Kristen Bell, and many others show up in ninety-nine other cities. The last city to get rescued was Chicago, and it required Oprah. After six days, Oprah was a no-show. On the fourth day, they organized a march that went round and round her studios. The next day they put on a singing and dancing presentation that went on all day and night. Then the sixth day, having endured harsh weather and sleeping in the rain, the more than five hundred participants surrounded her studio and stood in silence holding signs starting at 3:30 a.m. That morning Oprah walked out the doors of Harpo Studios, spoke with the organization's founders and invited the entire group to participate in a live broadcast segment that morning to her more than 20 million viewers. That attention got Invisible Children on *Larry King Live* and 232 other news outlets—to reach a total of more than 65 million people. A bill is currently moving through Congress supporting Invisible Children's efforts to save these children. The organization had already pulled off more than expected with the Rescue event, but the little extra gumption and steadfastness to capture that last city (and the attention of Oprah), gained Invisible Children its biggest advocate to date, multiplying its results many times over.

Find the line of expectation and then exceed it. Even when it comes to the small stuff—or maybe especially then. Whatever I think the dress standard is going to be for any event, for example, I always choose to go at least one step above it. When I am unsure of the attire, I always err on the side of dressing better than I suppose the occasion calls for. Simple, I know, but it's just one way I try to meet my standard to always do and be better than expected.

When I do keynotes for large companies, I spend a considerable amount of time preparing—learning about their organization, products, markets, and their expectations for my talk. My goal is always to significantly surpass what they expect, and I do this through tireless preparation. Doing better than expected becomes a big part of your reputation. Your reputation for excellence multiplies your results in the marketplace many times over.

I did some work with a CEO whose philosophy was to pay people, including his vendors and suppliers, a few days in advance of the contract commitment. I was always blown away when I received a check on the twenty-seventh of the month from him for next month's payment. When I asked him about it, he said the obvious, "It's the same money, but the surprise and good will it buys is immeasurable—why wouldn't you?"

This is one of the reasons why I admire Steve Jobs so much. Of all the sensational people we've featured on the cover of *SUCCESS*, Jobs is one of my favorites. Whatever your expectations are about the next Apple product launch, Jobs always has a little (or a lot of) something extra to WOW you. In the grand scheme of things, it might be only a minor addition, but even so, it's better than expected and multiplies the impression and response from his customers and deepens their loyalty. In a world where most things don't meet expectations, you can significantly accelerate your results and stand out from the pack by doing better than expected. I like the boldness of what Robert Schuller told us in his *SUCCESS* feature (December 2008), "I say no idea is worthwhile if it doesn't start with 'Wow!' "

Nordstrom is famous for this standard. When it comes to customer service, they always strive to do better than expected. Nordstrom has been known to take back an item that a customer bought more than a year ago, without a receipt, and in some cases, purchased at a different store! Why would they do that? Because they know exceeding expectations builds trust and creates customer loyalty. As a result, they've developed an extraordinary reputation that continues to attract attention. After all, I'm reminding you of it here. The *multiplier* keeps growing!

I challenge you to adopt these philosophies in your own life—in your daily habits, disciplines and routines. Giving a little more time, energy, or thought to your efforts won't just improve your results; it will multiply them. It takes very little extra to be EXTRAordinary. In all areas of your life, look for the multiplier opportunities where you can go a little further, push yourself a little harder, last a little longer, prepare a little better, and deliver a little bit more. Where can you do better and more than expected? When can you do the totally unexpected? Find as many opportunities for "WOW," and the level and speed of your accomplishments will astonish you... and everyone else around you.

Put the Compound Effect to Work for You

Summary Action Steps

↗ When do you hit your moments of truth (e.g., making prospecting calls, exercising, communicating with your spouse or kids)? Identify so you know when to push through to find new growth and where you can separate yourself from others and your old self.

↗ Find three areas in your life where you can you do "extra" (e.g., weight lifting reps, calls, recognition, sentiments of appreciation, etc.).

↗ Identify three areas in your life where you can beat the expectations. Where and how can you create "wow" moments?

↗ Identify three ways you can do the unexpected. Where can you differentiate from what is common, normal, or expected?

CONCLUSION

Learning without execution is useless. I didn't write this book for my own amusement (this is hard work!) or even to simply "motivate" you. Motivation without action leads to self-delusion. As I said in the introduction, the Compound Effect and the results it will manifest in your life are the real deal. Never again will you wish and hope that success will find you. The Compound Effect is a tool that, when combined with consistent, positive action, will make a real and lasting difference in your life. Let this book and its philosophy become your guide. Let the ideas and success strategies sink in and produce genuine, tangible, measurable outcomes for you. Whenever you realize small, seemingly innocuous poor habits have crept back into your life, take out this book. Whenever you fall off the wagon of consistency, take out this book. Whenever you want to reignite your motivation and bolster your why-power, take out this book. Every time you read this book, it entices Big Mo to pay a visit to your life.

Let me share with you what motivates me. My core value in life is significance. My desire is to make a positive difference in other people's lives. So to accomplish my goals, I need *you* to accomplish *your* goals. It is your testimonial of life-changing results I'm after. I want to receive your e-mail or letter, or to have you stop me in the airport next year (or even five or ten years from now), to tell me about the incredible results you've realized because of ideas you gained from this book. Only then will I know I have accomplished my goals, my objectives—that I am living up to my core values in life.

For you to get those results (and me, my testimonial), I know you have to take immediate action on your new insights and knowledge. Ideas uninvested are wasted. I don't want that to happen. It's now time to act on your new convictions. You now have the power, and I expect you to seize it!

You *are* ready to make dramatic improvements, right? Of course, the obvious answer is, "YES!" But you know by now that saying you're ready to make the necessary changes and actually making them isn't the same thing. To get different results, you're going to have to do things differently.

No matter where you are, or what year it is when you find this book, if I could, I'd ask you these simple questions: "Look back on your life five years ago. Are you *now* where you'd thought you'd be five years later? Have you kicked the bad habits you had vowed to kick? Are you in the shape you wanted to be? Do you have the cushy income, the enviable lifestyle, and the personal freedom you expected? Do you have the vibrant health, abundant loving relationships, and the world-class skills you'd intended to have by this point in your life?" If not, why? Simple—choices. It's time to make a new choice—choose to not let the next five years be a continuum of the last. Choose to change your life, once and for all.

Let's make the next five years of your life fantastically different than the last five! My hope is that you've now removed your blinders.

You know the truth about what it takes to earn success. You've got no more excuses. Like me, you too will refuse to be fooled by the latest gimmicks or become distracted by quick-fix enticements. You will stay focused on the simple but profound disciplines that will lead you in the direction of your desires. You know that success isn't easy or overnight. You understand that when you're committed to making moment-to-moment positive choices (despite the lack of visible or instant results), the Compound Effect *will* catapult you to heights that will astound you, bewilder your friends, family, and your competition. When you hold true to your why-power and stay consistent with your new behaviors and habits, momentum will carry you swiftly forward. And then, together, with that momentum and consistent, positive action, it will be impossible for the next five years to be more of the same. On the contrary, when you put the Compound Effect to work for you, you will experience a success I'm willing to bet you currently cannot imagine! It will be incredible.

I have one more valuable success principle to pass along to you. Whatever I want in life, I've found that the best way to get it is to focus my energy on giving to others. If I want to boost my confidence, I look for ways to help someone else feel more confident. If I want to feel more hopeful, positive, and inspired, I try to infuse that in someone else's day. If I want more success for myself, the fastest way to get it is to go about helping someone else obtain it.

The ripple effect of helping others and giving generously of your time and energy is that you become the biggest beneficiary of your personal philanthropy. As the first simple and small step I'd like you to take in improving the trajectory of your life, I ask you to try this philosophy in your own life. If you've found value in this book, if it's helped you in any way, consider giving a copy to five people whom you care about and want greater success for. The recipients could be relatives, friends, team members, vendors, your favorite local small-business owner, or someone you just met and would like to make a marked difference in their life. I know this sounds like it benefits me. It does. Remember, I am after the success testimonials. My goal is to make a difference in millions of people's lives, but to do that, I need your help. But I promise you this: ultimately, it will be you who benefits the most. Your helping someone else find the ideas to gain greater success is the first step toward you exercising them in your own life. At the same time you could make a marked difference in the life of someone else. This book could forever alter the course of someone's life… and it could be you who gives it to them. Without you, they might not ever find it.

Write down the five people you will give a copy of this book to:

1) _____

2) _____

3) _____

4) _____

5) _____

Thank you for honoring me with your valuable time! I look forward to reading your success story.

To *YOUR* success!

Darren Hardy

RESOURCE GUIDE

The Mentor Pack

This very special package includes Darren Hardy's top-selling *Living Your Best Year Ever* success planning system in workbook format, as well as Jim Rohn's extraordinary audio programs, *Challenge to Succeed*, *The Art of Exceptional Living*, and *Take Charge of Your Life*.

www.SUCCESS.com/MentorPack

Living Your Best Year Ever

Outlines the specific plan that Darren developed for himself, synthesizing hundreds of books, seminars, trials, errors and victories into the best and proven strategies on how to design, execute, stick to and achieve big goals.

www.SUCCESS.com/BestYearEver

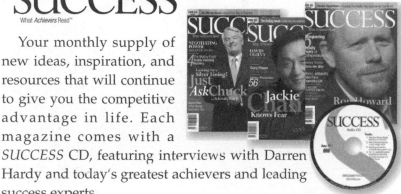

Gratitude Assessment

Three amazing people in my life are

1. _____
2. _____
3. _____

Three great things about my physical body are

1. _____
2. _____
3. _____

Three great things about my home and where I live are

1. _____
2. _____
3. _____

Three great things about where I work and what I do for a living are

1. _____
2. _____
3. _____

Three great gifts of unique talent and skill I have been given are

1. _____
2. _____
3. _____

Three great gifts of knowledge and experience I have been given are

1. _____
2. _____
3. _____

Three ways I have experienced "luck" in my life are

1. _____
2. _____
3. _____

Three ways in which my life is wealthy, abundant and prosperous are

1. _____
2. _____
3. _____

Get the complete, printable worksheet at www.TheCompoundEffect.com/free

Core Values Assessment

Your values are your GPS navigation system for life. Getting them defined and properly calibrated is one of the most important steps in redirecting your life toward your grandest vision. The below series of questions will help you evaluate and refine what is truly important to you and what matters most in life. Answer each question thoughtfully, and then I will help you select the top half-dozen values for your life.

Who is the person I respect most in life? What are their core values?

_____

_____

Who is my best friend, and what are his/her top three qualities?

_____

_____

If I could have more of any one quality instantly, what would it be?

_____

_____

What are three things I hate? (e.g., cruelty to animals, credit card companies, deforestation, etc.)

_____

_____

Which three people in the world do I dislike the most and why?

_____

_____

_____

Which personality trait, attribute or quality do people compliment me on the most?

_____

_____

What are the three most important values I want to pass on to my children?

_____

_____

_____

Get the complete, printable worksheet at www.TheCompoundEffect.com/free

Life Assessment

Face the truth

There are no wrong answers, there is no grade, no rating, not even an interpretation of your responses other than your own thoughtful assessment. Be honest and truthful with yourself. Even when the truthful response is a little embarrassing or painful, remember that no one else need ever see it and that you never succeed by deceiving yourself.

Rate the following on a scale of 1 to 5, 1 being Least True and 5 being Most True:

RELATIONSHIPS & FAMILY					
I spend at least 10 hours of focused time with my family each week.	1	2	3	4	5
I get together with friends at least once a week.	1	2	3	4	5
There is no one in my life that I haven't completely forgiven.	1	2	3	4	5
I am actively engaged in learning how to be a better spouse, parent and/or friend.	1	2	3	4	5
I actively look for ways to support and help advance the success of my friends and family.	1	2	3	4	5
I take complete responsibility for all relationship conflicts when they arise.	1	2	3	4	5
I easily trust those I live and work with.	1	2	3	4	5
I am 100% honest and open with all those I live and work with.	1	2	3	4	5
It is easy for me to commit to others and honor those commitments.	1	2	3	4	5
I recognize when I need support and am continually seeking help.	1	2	3	4	5
Total Score:					

PHYSICAL					
I do strength training at least 3x a week.	1	2	3	4	5
I do cardiovascular exercise at least 3x a week.	1	2	3	4	5
I do stretching and/or yoga type exercise at least 3x a week.	1	2	3	4	5
During a typical day, I watch no more than 1 hour of TV.	1	2	3	4	5
I eat breakfast (more than just coffee) every day.	1	2	3	4	5
I don't eat fast food, ever.	1	2	3	4	5
I spend time outside for at least 30 minutes a day, every day.	1	2	3	4	5
I have undisturbed sleep for at least 8 hours each night.	1	2	3	4	5
I don't drink more than 1 caffeinated beverage per day.	1	2	3	4	5
I drink at least 8 glasses of water per day	1	2	3	4	5
Total Score:					

Get the complete, printable worksheet at www.TheCompoundEffect.com/free

Habit Assessment

The magic comes from becoming the person you need to be in order to attract the people or results you wish to meet or achieve. Use the example below to determine the magic factor for achieving your goals.

EXAMPLE:

GOAL: Earn an extra $100,000 in income in 2010

General description of WHO I NEED TO BECOME:

- I am a disciplined master of time efficiency.
- I focus solely on high-payoff and high-productivity actions.
- I wake up an hour earlier and review my priority objectives each morning.
- I fuel my body properly and exercise four days a week so I am energetic and highly effective each work hour.
- I feed my mind ideas and inspiration that will support and bolster my passion.
- I surround myself with peers and mentors who elevate my expectations and prod me to rise to greater levels of discipline, commitment and achievement.
- I am a smart, confident and effective leader.
- I seek and cultivate the strength and greatness in everyone around me.
- I deliver excellence to my clients and continually find ways to 'wow' them, encouraging repeat transactions and abundant referrals.

New habits, disciplines or behaviors I need to START:

- Get up by 5am, feed my mind with positive material— 30 minutes reading and 30 minutes of audio of something inspirational and instructional every day
- 30 minutes of quiet thinking time
- 30 minutes of planning time, eating a healthy fiber and protein rich breakfast
- Exercise for at least 30 minutes three times a week
- Calling on 10 new major accounts per week, checking in, servicing and further developing 10 existing clients per week, planning each day the night before, remembering birthdays and anniversaries of employees and clients, following news, blogs and updates of target accounts…

Existing healthy habits, disciplines or behaviors I need to EXPAND:

Recognizing my teammates when they achieve, delegating administrative tasks, going into the office early, being prompt, professional dress…

Poor habits or behaviors I need to STOP:

- Watching two hours of TV at night and listening to news in the car
- Attending unproductive meetings and saying yes to projects in conflict with my highest priorities
- Gossiping with colleagues, complaining about the economy, the market, team members or customers
- Taking personal calls or spending time on Facebook or other personal social media sites during the day
- Eating after 7:30pm, more than one glass of wine at night, extended lunches without clients…

Top three modifications and how I will implement it into my daily routine:	
HABIT, BEHAVIOR OR DISCIPLINE	IMPLEMENTATION IN ROUTINE
Feed mind	Read 30 min first thing in morning while coffee brews. Listen to audio on commute to and from office.
Call on 10 new clients per week	Tues 2pm-5pm, Weds 10am-12pm, Thurs 1pm-4pm
Supportive associations	Join and commit to bi-weekly mastermind forum

Get the complete, printable worksheet at www.TheCompoundEffect.com/free

Weekly Rhythm Register

Weekly Rhythm Register

Behavior/Action	Mon	Tues	Weds	Thurs	Fri	Sat	Sun	Achieved	Goal	Net
							TOTAL			

Commitment is doing the thing you said you were going to do
long after the mood you said it in has left you.

Date Range: _____ – _____

Get the complete, printable worksheet at www.TheCompoundEffect.com/free

Input Influences

Assessing Your Input

Let's look at all the potential ways you are feeding your mind less-than-supportive input. Just put a zero if you don't do a particular activity.

Activity	Time Per Day	Per Week	Total per Year
Read newspaper			
Morning TV shows or news programs			
News radio in car			
Evening TV news			
TV news during day (CNN, etc.)			
News on Web site homepages			
RSS news feeds			
News, gossip blogs, Web sites, readers, etc.			
News magazines (*Newsweek*, *TIME*, etc.)			
Gossip magazines (*People*, *Vanity Fair*, etc.)			
Other sources for news, gossip and "social			
Sitcom or other TV viewing			
Less-than-life-affirming movie viewing			
Total			

List three ways you will cut or significantly limit your input of negative, fear mongering, worrisome, gossip or needless social commentary input via newspapers, TV, radio, magazines, Web sites or otherwise.

1. _____

2. _____

3. _____

Your Plan to Feed Your Mind

What are the ways you will proactively feed your mind positive, inspirational, abundant, prosperity-minded ideas, information and input?

1. _____

2. _____

3. _____

4. _____

5. _____

Get the complete, printable worksheet at www.TheCompoundEffect.com/free

Association Evaluator

Assessing Your Current Associations

This is about the amount of TIME you spend with people outside of your immediate household (spouse and kids) and your strict work interactions (those in your office, unless you spend time outside of work with them). Evaluate their level of success in each of the areas below.

Name	Physical	Financial	Business/ Profession	Mental/ Attitude	Spiritual/ Loving	Family	Relationships	Lifestyle	Average
1.									
2.									
3.									
4.									
5.									
Average									

Now, organize your associations into the following three categories: dissociations, limited associations and expanded associations.

Disassociations

Maybe you need to disassociate from someone in the chart above, or anyone else who is involved in your life to any degree, who has a negative influence on you—mentally, emotionally, attitudinally, physically or otherwise. These are people who have a negative effect on what you talk about, what you eat, drink, do, watch, listen to, etc.

Name
1.
2.
3.

Get the complete, printable worksheet at www.TheCompoundEffect.com/free

THE
COMPOUND
EFFECT

Enhanced Audiobook Also Available!

Take the next step in implementing the Compound Effect in all areas of your life. Read by Darren Hardy, this inspiring audiobook includes additional anecdotes and success strategies from some of today's greatest achievers. This special-edition version will motivate you to take action.

Also on TheCompoundEffect.com

- **Free downloadable resources and worksheets** that will help you put the power of the Compound Effect to work in your life.
- **Share *The Compound Effect* with others in your life.** Special discounted pricing is available for bulk orders of the book.

More on Darren Hardy

To have Darren Hardy speak to your organization about the principles found in *The Compound Effect* or other success insights, e-mail **speaker@SUCCESS.com**.

For more information about Darren, visit: **www.DarrenHardy.com**. Connect with Darren and a community of like-minded, ambitious achievers online:

www.twitter.com/DarrenHardy

www.facebook.com/DarrenHardyfan

http://DarrenHardy.SUCCESS.com